Inside
WikiLeaks

CROWN PUBLISHERS

NEW YORK

Inside
WikiLeaks

My Time with
JULIAN ASSANGE
at the World's Most
Dangerous Website

Daniel Domscheit-Berg

with Tina Klopp

TRANSLATED INTO ENGLISH BY JEFFERSON CHASE

CROWN and the Crown colophon are registered trademarks
of Random House, Inc.

Originally published in paperback in Germany as *Inside WikiLeaks:
Meine Zeit bei der gefährlichsten Website der Welt* by Econ, an imprint
of Ullstein Buchverlage GmbH, Berlin. Copyright © 2011 by Daniel
Domscheit-Berg, copyright © Ullstein Buchverlage GmbH, Berlin.

Library of Congress Cataloging-in-Publication Data
is available upon request.

ISBN 978-0-307-95191-5
eISBN 978-0-307-95193-9

Printed in the United States of America

JACKET DESIGN BY SABINE WIMMER, BERLIN

10 9 8 7 6 5 4 3 2 1

First American Edition

To the First Amendment
and those defending the
world's most precious bastion
of freedom of speech

Contents

Author's Note

WHEN I joined WikiLeaks in 2007, I found myself involved in a project devoted above all to one goal: subjecting the power that was exercised behind closed doors to public scrutiny. The idea of using an Internet platform to create transparency where it was most resisted was as simple as it was brilliant.

Over the course of my time with Julian Assange at WikiLeaks, I would experience firsthand how power and secrecy corrupt people. As the months passed, WikiLeaks developed in a direction that dismayed core members of the team and led us to leave the project in September 2010. I was confident that the diplomatic, almost reticent criticism I voiced at the time would cause people to question the power of WikiLeaks and the chief figure behind it, as is the case with other organizations.

In fact, the opposite happened. Small segments of the public around the world, people who had been acquainted with the topic for a while, did begin to criticize what WikiLeaks had turned into, but their questions were drowned out in the hype surrounding the platform for leaking confidential documents and its founder.

Julian Assange and WikiLeaks, bound inextricably to each other, became a pop-culture phenomenon.

That was due primarily to the informational vacuum at the heart of a secretive organization whose motto is transparency. Now, like so many of the people to whom we gave a platform for revelations, I have decided to make inside information public. This isn't a decision I have taken lightly. For a long time, I was torn between feelings of loyalty and my own moral standards.

At WikiLeaks we often used to say that only an accurate historical record can enable a true understanding of the world. I have decided to do my part toward that end with this book.

DANIEL DOMSCHEIT-BERG
Berlin
January 2011

A WikiLeaks Timeline

OCTOBER 4, 2006: WikiLeaks.org is registered as a domain name

DECEMBER 2006: First publications

JANUARY 2007: WikiLeaks announces 1.2 million documents waiting to be processed and published

NOVEMBER 2007: WikiLeaks publishes the Guantánamo Bay handbooks

DECEMBER 2007: Daniel meets Julian at the 24th Chaos Communication Congress (24C3) in Berlin

JANUARY 2008: WikiLeaks publishes hundreds of documents about the Cayman Islands subsidiary of the Swiss banking house Julius Bär

FEBRUARY 2008: Julius Bär sues Dynadot (the registry of WikiLeaks.org), loses the injunction it obtained to shut down the WikiLeaks site, and then withdraws the suit

MARCH 2008: WikiLeaks publishes the Scientology handbooks

MAY 2008: WikiLeaks publishes the first American fraternity handbook

June 2008: WikiLeaks publishes documents from the "Memorandum of Understanding" in Kenya

June 2008: Global Voices Summit in Budapest

September 2008: WikiLeaks publishes e-mails from the private account of Sarah Palin

November 2008: WikiLeaks publishes a membership list of the far-right British National Party

November 2008: WikiLeaks publishes a report by the Oscar Legal Aid Foundation about political killings carried out by Kenyan police

December 2008: WikiLeaks publishes German secret service documents about corruption in Kosovo in cooperation with German media

December 2008: WikiLeaks publishes the 2008 Human Terrain Team handbook

December 2008: Daniel and Julian hold their first official lecture at the Chaos Communication Congress (25C3)

January 2009: Daniel quits his job and begins working full-time for WL

February 2009: WikiLeaks publishes more than 6,700 Congressional Research Service reports

February 2009: WikiLeaks inadvertently publishes the e-mail addresses of WL donors

March 2009: WikiLeaks publishes the database of supporters of US senator Norm Coleman

April 2009: International Journalism Festival in Perugia, Italy

June 2009: WikiLeaks receives an Amnesty International Media Award

JULY 2009: WikiLeaks publishes a list of the biggest debtors to the Icelandic Kaupthing Bank

AUGUST 2009: Hacking At Random (HAR) conference in Vierhouten, Netherlands

SEPTEMBER 2009: WikiLeaks receives a prize from Ars Electronica in the category "Digital Communities"

OCTOBER 2009: WikiLeaks publishes a second membership list of the British National Party

NOVEMBER 2009: WikiLeaks publishes the 9/11 pager messages

NOVEMBER 2009: WikiLeaks publishes the investigators' reports about a major German pharmaceutical company

NOVEMBER 2009: WikiLeaks publishes the Toll Collect contracts

NOVEMBER 2009: WikiLeaks publishes the e-mail correspondence of David Irving

NOVEMBER 2009: WikiLeaks initiates the idea of a free haven for the media, leading to the Icelandic Modern Media Initiative (IMMI)

DECEMBER 2009: WikiLeaks publishes field reports concerning the bombing of two tanker trucks in Kunduz

DECEMBER 23, 2009: WikiLeaks goes offline

DECEMBER 27, 2009: Daniel and Julian talk about the future of WikiLeaks at the Chaos Communication Congress (26C3)

JANUARY 5, 2010: WikiLeaks begins work in Iceland on the Icelandic Modern Media Initiative (IMMI)

APRIL 5, 2010: WikiLeaks publishes the "Collateral Murder" video

MAY 26, 2010: Bradley Manning is arrested

JULY 26, 2010: WikiLeaks publishes the Afghan War Diaries

JULY 30, 2010: WikiLeaks posts the encrypted insurance file

AUGUST 20, 2010: WikiLeaks publishes documents concerning the planning of the Love Parade in Duisburg, Germany

AUGUST 20, 2010: A warrant for Julian's arrest is issued, then withdrawn in Sweden

AUGUST 26, 2010: Julian suspends Daniel

SEPTEMBER 14, 2010: Daniel repairs a malfunctioning mail server

SEPTEMBER 15, 2010: Daniel and others leave WikiLeaks

SEPTEMBER 17, 2010: OpenLeaks.org is registered as a domain name

OCTOBER 22, 2010: WikiLeaks publishes the Iraq War Logs

NOVEMBER 28, 2010: WikiLeaks publishes US diplomatic cables

DECEMBER 1, 2010: Interpol issues a Red Notice international warrant for Julian's arrest

DECEMBER 7, 2010: Julian turns himself in to police in London

DECEMBER 14, 2010: Julian is released on bail

DECEMBER 30, 2010: Daniel presents OpenLeaks at the Chaos Communication Congress (27C3)

Inside
WikiLeaks

I STARE at the monitor. The screen is black with green letters. A couple of posts react to the lines I wrote. I ignore them. I've already typed my last words. There's nothing left to say. It's over. Forever.

Julian was no longer present in the chat room. At least, he hadn't answered. Perhaps he was sitting silently in front of his computer, apathetic, shocked, or enraged, in Sweden or wherever he was keeping himself at the moment. I didn't know. I only knew I was never going to talk to him again.

The bar on the corner had discharged the last of its guests into the night. I heard them cheerfully heading toward the nighttime streetcar stop. It was approaching two a.m. on September 15, 2010.

I left my laptop on my desk and collapsed into a pile of cushions in the corner of my living room. I picked up a novel by Neil Gaiman and Terry Pratchett and started reading. What else was one supposed to do in a situation like this? What would other people do?

I read for hours. At some point I fell asleep, still in my jeans and sweater, with woolen slippers from my grandmother on my feet. The book fell to the floor. I remember the title: *Good Omens*.

How do you walk out of your job when the place where you work is the whole world? When there are no colleagues around to give a farewell handshake? When two hastily typed lines, in green letters, have burned all your bridges? When no one even gives you a swift kick in the ass to send you on your way?

"You're suspended," Julian had written me weeks ago.

As if he alone were the only one who could decide. Now it was finally over.

When I awoke the next morning, everything looked normal. My wife, my son, our usual household mess—everything was exactly as it had been, and the sun was shining through our living room window at the same familiar angle. But it all felt different. A part of my life had been transformed from a promising future to a past that was dead and gone, never to be recaptured.

I had broken off contact with the people with whom I had shared the past three years of my life and for whom I had given up my regular job and neglected my girlfriend at the time, family, and friends.

For years, the chat room at WikiLeaks.org had been my central channel to the outside world. Sometimes, when I was working on an important publication, it was my only channel. I was never again going to log myself in. Weeks earlier, Julian had blocked access to my mail account. He had even threatened me with the police. But instead of signing the confidentiality agreement others had encouraged me to put my name to, I am writing this book.

We used to be best friends, Julian and I—or, at least, something like friends. Today, I'm not sure whether he even knows the concept. I'm not sure of anything anymore. Sometimes I hate him so much that I'm afraid I'd resort to physical violence if our paths ever cross again. Then I think that he needs my help. That's absurd, after everything that's happened. Never in my life have I known such an extreme person as Julian Assange.

So imaginative. So energetic. So brilliant.

So paranoid, so power-hungry, so megalomanic.

I believe I can say we spent the best years of our lives together, and I know we can never go back. Now that a few months have passed and my emotions have calmed down, I think that everything is all right the way it is. But I also freely admit that I wouldn't trade the past few years for anything in the world. I'm afraid that, given the choice, I'd do it all over again.

The things I've experienced! I looked into many an abyss and played with the levers of power. I've understood how Scientology, high-level corruption, money laundering, the peddling of political influence, and the waging of war actually function. I've telephoned via Cryptophone to maintain security, traveled the world, and been embraced by grateful people on the street in Iceland. One day I ate cake with the investigative reporter Seymour Hersh; the next, I sat on the bus with Germany's Labor minister, Ursula von der Leyen; and on the third I watched us make headlines in the nightly news. I played a role in parliamentarians' decision not to pass a badly written law on censorship in Germany, and I was onboard when they enacted a fine piece of legislation in Iceland.

Julian Assange, the founder of WikiLeaks, was my best friend. The site made him into a pop star, one of the most intriguingly zany media figures in the world. Unfortunately, his brand of zaniness is also dangerous, and I noticed that fact too late.

What connected Julian and me was the belief in a better world. In the world we dreamed of, there would be no more bosses or hierarchies, and no one could achieve power by withholding from the others the knowledge needed to act as an equal player. That was the idea for which we fought. It was the project that we started together and watched grow with enormous pride.

In the past few years, WikiLeaks has gotten huge—much bigger than I would have ever thought possible in 2007, when, almost accidentally, driven by curiosity, I joined the project. It made two pale-faced computer freaks, whose intelligence would have otherwise gone unnoticed, into public figures who put fear into the hearts of the politicians, business leaders, and military commanders of this world. They probably had nightmares about us. A lot of them probably wished that we had never been born.

That had felt good.

There were times when I could hardly sleep, in anticipation of what tomorrow would bring. There was a period every morning in which something happened that I was convinced would make the world a little bit better. I'm not being ironic. I really believed this. Better yet, I still believe in the idea. I'm convinced the project itself was brilliant. Perhaps it was too brilliant to work the first time around.

During my last few months with WikiLeaks, I also slept badly, but this time it was from fear and not anticipation. Every morning I expected that the next catastrophe would strike, that everything would come crashing down around our ears, something major would go wrong and a source would be put in danger. Or that Julian would launch another attack against me or one of the others who had previously been his closest confidants.

Julian wrote an introduction to the most recent set of leaks, "Cablegate." The leak, he said, illustrated the contradictions between public appearances and what goes on behind closed doors. People, he asserted, have a right to know what happens behind the scenes.

You can't put it any better than that. And it's high time to look behind the curtains of WikiLeaks itself.

1

The First Meeting

I FIRST heard about WikiLeaks in September 2007. A buddy of mine told me about it in a chat. At the time, we were regular readers of cryptome.org, the whistle-blower website run by John Young. It had made the headlines, among other things because lists of agents working for MI6, the British secret service, had been published there in 1999 and 2005. Cryptome published documents from people who wanted to reveal secrets without running the risk of being branded traitors. It was the same idea WikiLeaks was based on.

Ironically, many people initially assumed that some international secret service was actually behind WikiLeaks—that the platform was a so-called honeypot, a trap offering people a platform for revealing secrets where they would actually be arrested if they uploaded anything controversial. The predominant attitude was one of mistrust.

Then in November 2007, the handbooks from Guantánamo Bay, the "Camp Delta Standard Operating Procedures," appeared on WikiLeaks. They revealed that the United States was violating internees' human rights and the Geneva Conventions at their military base in Cuba. Three things were immediately clear to me.

One: It was absurd to think that WikiLeaks was a secret-service front.

Two: The project had the potential to become much, much bigger than Cryptome.

Three: WikiLeaks was a great idea. For people who'd been active from the beginning in these sorts of communities, the Internet was not a global sea of data, but a village. If I needed a reliable opinion about something, I knew where to ask. So that's what I did, and the answer was always: "WL? It's a fantastic idea." That encouraged me to learn more. I logged in to a chat room, which still exists today on the WikiLeaks site, and started making contacts. I got the sense immediately that these people were the same as me. They were interested in the same issues. They worked the same ungodly hours. They talked about social problems and believed that the Internet offered previously unimaginable solutions. After a day of this, I asked if there was anything I could do. At first I got no answer. I was confused and a bit insulted. Still, I kept participating in the chat.

"Still interested in a job?" came a message two days later. It was Julian Assange.

"Sure! Tell me what," I typed in response.

At first Julian gave me a couple of menial tasks: cleaning up the Wiki site, making formats cohere, and revising some content. I was still a long way from dealing with any sensitive documents. Then I had the idea of introducing WikiLeaks into the program of the 24th Chaos Communication Congress, the legendary meeting of the hacker and computing scene sponsored by the

Chaos Computer Club, a well-respected organization of technology activists in Germany. The congress takes place every year in Berlin between Christmas and New Year's Day.

I knew little about how WikiLeaks was run internally. I didn't even know how many others besides me were involved or what sort of technical infrastructure the project had. When I thought about it, I imagined WikiLeaks as a midsized organization with a well-organized team, robust technology, and servers across the globe.

Back then, I had a regular job. I was responsible for network design and security for a large American company that did IT work for civilian and military clients and had its German headquarters in the town of Rüsselsheim. My employer and I had a tacit agreement that I wouldn't have to deal with any weapons companies, so I worked primarily for GM, Opel, and a number of airlines. Anyone who books an overseas flight these days will probably use the technology that I developed.

I earned around 50,000 euros a year—too little for what I was doing, but I didn't care. I was active in the open source community. I worked longer hours than the required forty a week and was always experimenting with new solutions. What I did was generally appreciated within the company.

My coworkers and I constantly thought up the sort of pranks that technically gifted people use to keep up their spirits in companies like ours. To protest the quality of the coffee, we manipulated the menus of the supposedly economical coffee machines so that they needed constant maintenance. I would regularly send e-mails to a short-tempered colleague from an address on the company server called god@eds.de. I enjoyed watching him becoming ever more enraged and would send him follow-up e-mails with statements like "God says you shouldn't get so excited."

I lived nearby in the small city of Wiesbaden, and my girl-friend at the time, a very beautiful young woman, worked as a secretary for the company. All in all, I was content with, but hardly euphoric about, my life. My days were full and varied, but there was room for something more.

After our falling-out, Julian reportedly said that I would have been nothing without WikiLeaks—that I only got involved with WL because I had nothing better to do with my life.

He was right. WL is the best thing that has ever happened to me, although I hardly suffered from extreme boredom before I joined it. I had a server in my kitchen that ate up 8,500 kilowatt hours of electricity annually, I was constantly tinkering around with networks, and I met up with people at the local branch of the Chaos Club. Still, my heart was only half in these things. Something was missing in my life in those years. A purpose. A task that would truly inspire me and make me give up everything else.

The Chaos Computer Club was an important point of social connection for me, and the space where the club met in Berlin was always one of the first addresses I visited whenever I was in the German capital. How can I describe what I liked about the people there? All of them were complete curmudgeons. Very creative, clever, but somewhat gruff individuals who had no time for superficial social niceties. But what they lacked in grace, they compensated for ten times over in loyalty, once they had accepted you into their ranks. All of them were occupied with something round the clock, even if outsiders were often unable to understand precisely what it was and why they were doing it. And every club member was an expert in something, be it freeware, electronic music, visual art, hacking, IT security, data protection, or light shows. The spectrum of people's interests was enormous.

The club also had a decisive advantage compared with many other communities. It had a physical location. That's something of inestimable importance for people who spend a lot of their time in digital spaces. In the club, you could sit together and talk over problems face-to-face. You could even, as I would discover later, spend the night on one of their many couches if you'd gotten yourself into a jam. The club made sure that its members met up at regular intervals, for example at the annual congress, which took place at the Berliner Congress Center (bcc) in the heart of the city.

In early December 2007, Julian sent me a message in the chat room: "We'll see each other in Berlin. I'm looking forward to the lecture."

My first thought was, Fuck. I hope it's going to happen. It wasn't clear until right before the start of the congress whether Julian's address would even take place. I'd done my best to arrange it for him, but the deadline for submitting proposals had expired in August. On the other hand, I was afraid that I would have pulled all my strings in Berlin only to see no one from WL turn up.

As was his habit, Julian was set to arrive last-minute, and it turned out that no lecture had been scheduled for him. To this day, I have no idea whether he'd sent them the draft they had asked him for. It's possible that back then no one understood what WikiLeaks was and how significant it could be. It's also possible that many of the club members viewed WL with a critical eye and decided not to include Julian in the main program. Early on in Germany, we had encountered a lot of resistance from data-protection activists. "Protect Private Data—Use Public Data"—that was the slogan. We operated in a gray area, and that provoked a lot of discussion.

In any case, Julian was not part of the official program. The congress organizers had merely granted us permission to stage a small presentation in one of the workshop spaces. Julian had already started kicking up a fuss at reception because he refused to pay the entrance fee. He assumed he would be admitted free of charge because he was speaking, but the volunteer ticket takers saw things differently. And he wasn't present on the official list of speakers, so they wanted him to pay 70 euros. Julian simply deposited his backpack in the pressroom and took over the space. Julian usually traveled with only a backpack, which contained all his worldly possessions.

The pressroom was a modest-sized room with a dark tiled floor and a row of tables behind movable, separating walls. It was located on the second floor, all the way at the end of a hallway, and the blinds were usually drawn even in the daytime. Normally, journalists would use the room as a quiet space where they could work on their laptops in peace. Julian immediately comman-deered it for his daily routine, sitting for hours at a time in front of his computer, typing loudly.

If others asked if they could have the space for a quarter of an hour to conduct a radio interview or something, Julian flatly refused to make way—or even to type a bit more quietly.

Although the congress organizers tried every evening to get rid of their stubborn guest, Julian insisted that he had booked the space, and that it was well within his rights to spend the nights there as well. And he did, presumably wrapped up in his jacket and sleeping atop one of the tables since the tiles were far too cold to doze off on.

My first thought upon seeing him was: Cool guy. He was wearing olive-green cargo pants, a white shirt, and a green woolen vest from a suit—attire that distinguished him from the rest of the congress participants. The way he walked was both energetic and carefree, and he took huge strides. When he went up the stairs, the floorboards would vibrate. Occasionally, he would take a running start and glide across the freshly waxed floor in his well-worn boots. Or he'd slide down the banister, almost falling head over heels when he got to the bottom. It was fun watching him.

We met for the first time face-to-face by the spiral staircase on the second floor of the bcc. The congress was really full that day. Latecomers were fruitlessly begging for admission downstairs at reception, and the previous attendance record of 3,000 had been shattered. Masses of people were pushing their way, chatting all the while, through the hallways. Sometimes there were logjams of a quarter of an hour just to advance twenty meters. On the second floor, things were somewhat more relaxed. There was a leather sofa with a view of Alexanderplatz, eastern Berlin's main city square. This was to become our meeting point for the next couple of days. Whenever one of us had to go to the bathroom or get something to eat, the other would guard our things. If one of the congress visitors seemed to be eyeing our possessions, I'd bare my teeth at him.

We talked for hours. Then we would simply sit side by side, saying nothing, Julian absently working away at his computer.

I don't know what Julian was expecting when he came to Berlin. I wasn't particularly happy with the basement room we had been allocated for his presentation, but it turned out we were lucky it was small. Fewer than twenty people showed up at the lecture, and none of the more familiar faces within the club, as I noted to my dismay. I couldn't understand why no one seemed interested in this topic.

I sat up front on the right and observed Julian as he talked about WL in his friendly Australian accent. He wore the same clothes every day. The gleaming white shirt that had so impressed me when we first met lost some of its shine as time went on. If Julian was disappointed by the small number of listeners he attracted, he didn't let it show. He spoke for forty-five minutes, and afterward, when three people in the audience wanted to know more, he patiently answered their questions.

I felt a bit sorry for him that so few people had wanted to hear his lecture. He had paid for the trip out of his own pocket. When I turned around to look at the audience, I saw bewilderment in some of the faces. Later, his lectures would become much easier to follow, with a lot more examples. At the time, though, he still spoke very theoretically. Julian was truly tireless in his attempts to get audiences excited about his ideas.

Yet even though most people didn't know what to make of WL, in the months that followed, Julian and I would keep talking about the project to anyone who was prepared to listen for a few minutes. Even if there were only three of them. Today, the whole world knows us. Back then, every individual counted.

When the three people had asked their questions, Julian gathered his things, went back to the couch on the second floor, and reimmersed himself in his work.

I learned after the fact that there'd been a lot of trouble with the organizers, and Julian had quarreled with many of my acquaintances. For months after Julian's appearance, the club—my second home—remained skeptical about WikiLeaks. I always asked myself why that was.

In any case, Julian had made a huge impression on me.

This lanky Australian was someone who didn't let anyone boss him around or stop him from pursuing his work. He was also well read and had strong opinions about a number of topics. For example, he had a completely different view of the hacker community that I held in such regard. He thought they were "useless" idiots. That was typical of him. He was always judging people on their "usefulness," however he defined that category in a given situation. In his eyes, even particularly gifted hackers were idiots if they didn't apply their talents toward a larger goal.

Even back then I thought that his uncompromising personality and extreme opinions, which he would simply spit out undiplomatically, would put him at odds with a lot of people.

There was so much to plan and discuss, though, that I didn't have the time to keep analyzing the character of my new acquaintance. I didn't ask myself back then whether his behavior was normal or not. I didn't ask myself whether I could trust Julian or whether he might get me in trouble. On the contrary, I was somewhat flattered that he was interested in working with me. For me, Julian Assange was not only the founder of WL but also the hacker known as Mendax, a member of the famous International Subversives, one of the greatest hackers in the world, and the coauthor/researcher (with Suelette Dreyfus) of *Underground: Tales of Hacking, Madness and Obsession from the Electronic Frontier*—a highly respected book among connoisseurs. We hit it off right from the start.

He asked me very few personal questions. I think he respected me as someone who had said straightaway that he'd like to help and then showed commitment. That was probably more than what he had gotten from most other people at that point.

Soon I was able to experience this phenomenon for myself. Every time we published something, a few more volunteers would appear, saying, "We'd like to support WikiLeaks." But even when we gave them something concrete to do, only one out of a hundred, if even that, would ever get back in touch. I handed out the same tasks and wrote the same explanations hundreds of times, but it never amounted to anything. I think Julian had already been through this. And that's why he was glad to find an ally.

What's more, WikiLeaks quickly established a bond between us. We believed in the same ideals. We were equals—at least, that's the way I felt. Julian may have founded WikiLeaks, and he may have had more experience than I did, but right from the start I had the feeling that we were a pretty awesome team.

2

David vs. the Bears

IT was in January 2008—I'd only been onboard at WikiLeaks for a few months—that the first publications I'd been directly involved in appeared. Someone had uploaded a massive jumble of figures and calculations, organigrams, workflow documents, and contracts onto our digital mailbox. What significance did they have? It took Julian and me a couple of days to get an overview of the material. Hundreds of pages contained internal correspondence from the Julius Bär Bank, one of the largest private financial institutions in Switzerland. Now, as everyone knows, people don't always deposit money with Swiss bank accounts because of the quality of the clean Alpine air. From the documents, it was apparent that enormous amounts of money had been shielded from tax authorities. The material was full of concrete examples. We were talking about sums between $5 million and $100 million per client. The tax revenues not paid by dozens of exorbitantly wealthy individuals would have probably been enough to fund a dozen social programs.

The sinister elegance was shocking, especially because it was legal. A complex system of subsidiaries and financial transactions ensured that the money was well hidden on the Cayman Islands. I was impressed by the intelligence of the people who had thought this up.

We continued to do background research, wrote a summary, and posted everything in unadulterated form on the Internet. Then we issued a press release. Julian and I were really curious what the reaction would be. It was Monday, January 14, 2008.

Tuesday was staff-meeting day for me at my job. That entailed sitting with fifteen to twenty others in a claustrophobic conference room, breathing in stale air, and staring at Excel charts. The minute hand on the clock seemed as though it had been glued in place. Every five minutes, I stole a glance at my cell phone to see whether there was anything about WikiLeaks on Google News. I knew something was going to happen. What I didn't know was when.

Normally, the operators of websites want to know who is surfing their pages and what buttons get clicked. But we didn't have the technical setup for that. It would have contradicted Wiki-Leaks's principle of anonymity. So we never knew if anyone had looked at our material or not.

When my boss finally ended the meeting, I packed my things and sprinted out of the building. On my way home, I bought some meat, potatoes, and cauliflower in the organic grocery around the corner. Back in my apartment, a one-bedroom garden apartment with all the rooms branching off from a single gloomy hallway, I tossed my groceries on the kitchen counter and started my two laptops. There it was: the first reaction to our revelations about Julius Bär. The initial salvo in our battle against the powerful.

Our trial by fire. It arrived on January 15, 2008, at 8:30 p.m. It was time to buckle our seat belts. The ride was about to commence.

The sender was an attorney from a law firm based in California. Normally, the firm represents Hollywood stars. In an arrogant tone, the lawyer demanded that we name the source of our documents and remove them from the site.

"Holy fuck," Julian wrote. "Look at that."

"We'll destroy them," I typed back.

Julian and I always chatted. We never phoned. The messages that went back and forth in the next few hours between somewhere in the world and Wiesbaden, between Julian and me, were full of exclamation points and profanity.

While I peeled the potatoes, boiled the cauliflower, and braised the meat, Julian and I brainstormed about how to proceed. I wasn't worried that something bad could happen, that we might be arrested or that the material could be confiscated. We were out to stir up trouble. Official letters from courts and government authorities are always written as if their sole goal is to elicit maximum feelings of powerlessness and frustration in the addressee. This time we'd see who would come out on the short end. It was our first test of whether the system we'd invented, so brilliant in theory, would prove itself in practice.

We replied, asking the lawyer to be more specific. When we knew which client he was talking about, we would appoint the best lawyer in our legal arsenal to handle the case.

In reality, of course, we were light-years away from having a pool of attorneys at our beck and call. To be precise, we were in contact with one female attorney who had offered us her services for free. Her name was Julie Turner. She was from Texas, and it was a few days before we could get in touch with her. But to the outside world, we always pretended to have a huge legal department. My pseudonym was Daniel Schmitt. That wasn't particularly creative—it was the name of my cat. But I hoped it would be good enough to keep the private detectives at bay. We had heard from other people that big banking houses didn't shy away from hiring a detective agency to shadow anyone who made their lives uncomfortable. I had no desire to be spied upon.

Since the Julius Bär leak, I've been stuck with my pseudonym. The press knew me only as Daniel Schmitt.

In the next couple of days, I tried to work as much as possible from home. Around noon, I'd grab an old laptop, hastily wave to the boss, and mutter something about "trial runs" before heading back to my apartment. Whenever my cell phone would ring at work, I'd flee to the storeroom on the ninth floor.

It wasn't long before further e-mails arrived. A number of American civil rights groups had visited our site. What we had done spoke to their core interests: protecting informants and freedom of the press. One of the most common and hotly debated problems was that employees who wanted to reveal wrongdoing in their companies were often prevented from doing so by restrictive contracts with confidentiality agreements. The whistle-blower debate was much more advanced in the United States than in Germany, where people tended to see those who revealed company secrets as snitches rather than heroes in the cause of freedom of information.

In the beginning, it looked as though our adversaries would win. The opposition's lawyers succeeded in getting an emergency injunction from a California court. The suit was filed in California because that was where the WikiLeaks.org domain was then registered. They had argued that "company secrets" had been "stolen by a former employee" who had violated a "written confidentiality agreement." The judge ruled in their favor. The WikiLeaks.org page was taken offline. They had deleted us, or so they thought. But they weren't aware of another part of the WikiLeaks principle: When you took down one page from the Internet, twenty more would pop up in different locations to take its place. It was virtually impossible to take us off the Internet.

What followed was a global storm of outrage. Our telephones were ringing off the hook. Journalists from a number of different countries wanted to talk to us, and it took days to answer all the e-mails. Because of the time differences involved, sleep was almost out of the question. The media produced countless articles and programs about the Julius Bär case.

The journalists were clever enough to point out the approximately two hundred websites where WikiLeaks was still accessible. The *New York Times* devoted several articles to the case and published our IP address in one of them. The crowning moment was a headline on CBS News: FREEDOM OF SPEECH HAS A NUMBER. It was the WikiLeaks IP address: 88.80.13.160. We had hit the big time.

That's how we became so widely known within the space of just a few days in early 2008. Without Julius Bär, it never would have happened so quickly. In the aftermath, we received lots of encouragement, offers of help, and new documents. Never before in my life had things developed at such a breakneck pace.

The icing on the cake, though, was that we were able to stand up to the arrogant attorneys. After ten days or so, the judge revised his decision, and the site was back online. One of the main reasons was public pressure. One week after that, Julius Bär dropped its legal complaint. Recently I read somewhere that by 2010, according to European investigations on tax evasion, the flow of money to the bank had declined drastically.

Incidentally, there's never been another lawsuit against Wiki-Leaks.

We published the entire correspondence that went back and forth between us and the lawyers. The damage that Julius Bär suffered was significantly greater than what it would have been had the bank simply let the documents be published without complaint.

Various names appeared in our correspondence with Julius Bär's attorneys, but even at the best of times, never more than a handful of people were charged with important tasks. To be honest, a lot of the time it was just Julian and me. When "Thomas Bellman" or "Leon from the tech department" answered an e-mail and promised to forward a request on to our legal services, it was usually just me. Julian, too, used a host of pseudonyms. I am always asked to help people get in contact with other people who were involved in the project. I'm glad to pass on e-mail addresses, but even today I don't know whether some of the names are real people or alter egos of Julian Assange. "Jay Lim," for instance, is responsible for legal questions. Jay Lim? Someone Chinese, maybe? I've never met him. Nor did I ever have any contact with Chinese dissidents who, as rumor had it, were involved in setting up WikiLeaks.

For too long, we had only a single server, even though Julian and I knew that we had to make it seem otherwise to the public. We had to give the impression that we had a broad infrastructure. When the server went down, people thought we'd been hit by a cyberattack or been censored. The truth was, our technology was junk. Or we'd been unprofessional or neglected something important. If our adversaries had known that WikiLeaks was just two loudmouthed young men working with an antiquated server, they might have had the chance to stop our meteoric rise. Or at least to slow us down.

At the 26C3, the Chaos Communication Congress in December 2009, Julian and I attended a lecture about a new program for analyzing literature. The speakers described how easy it was to establish that various texts came from one and the same author. Like a form of handwriting, every individual is distinguished by recurrent stylistic elements, vocabulary, and syntax so that his authorship is unmistakable.

I nudged Julian with my foot. We exchanged glances and started giggling. If someone had run WikiLeaks documents through such a program, he would have discovered that the same two people were behind all the various press releases, document summaries, and correspondence issued by the project. The official number of volunteers we had was also, to put it mildly, grotesquely exaggerated. Even in the early days, we claimed that several thousand volunteers and hundreds of assistants supported us. This wasn't perhaps a direct falsehood, but that number included everyone who had signed up for our mailing list. These were people who had gotten in touch with us at some point with the vague promise of supporting the project. But they didn't do anything at all. They were just names. Not even names, really, just numbers.

Never during my first months of working for WikiLeaks did I realize this was the case. At most I asked myself why I so rarely met anyone besides Julian or heard about someone else taking care of this or that. These suspicions were reinforced by the fact that everyone who wrote e-mails had the same e-mail client as Julian. But I would never have confronted him about this. On the contrary, when I finally did realize how few people really were involved, my sense of being invaluable grew. And it motivated me to think that so few people could set such great things in motion.

Leaking the Julius Bär documents brought a certain Ralf Schneider* into our lives, a German citizen whose name was among those of the big tax evaders identified by the whistle-blower. At some point, Schneider sent us an e-mail, writing that, while he would love to have a few million to deposit in secret accounts in Switzerland, this was a case of mistaken identity. I was shocked.

The information about the individuals involved in the Julius Bär scandal came from our source. Whoever had provided us with the documents had wanted to help us categorize and understand them, so he had included some background information he had researched about the bank's clients. In the case of Ralf Schneider, he'd made a mistake. He'd confused the German with a Swiss who had a similar name. So we published the information about a possible mistake just as we did with the material provided by our source. On the site we wrote, "According to three independent sources, this document, the summary and some of

*Denotes that the name has been changed.

the commentary are false or misleading. WikiLeaks is investigating the matter." Three independent sources? That sounded good. Unfortunately it was made up.

One might ask here why we didn't simply delete the man's name. We decided against that because it was common for people connected to something negative to demand that we immediately remove their names. We wanted to investigate these cases before making any corrections.

Schneider had legitimate reason for being upset. When people Googled "Ralf Schneider," the first hit they saw was about him being involved in the tax evasion scandal. He was able to show, however, that other details from the documents didn't match him at all. "I do not have, nor did I ever have an account with the Julius Bär bank," he wrote to us. "I don't own a house on Mallorca, nor do I maintain a bank account on the Cayman Islands, and I don't live abroad. I have already instructed my attorney to file a charge of slander with the public prosecutor's office."

We didn't want to change the original documents provided by our source, but preferred instead to use commentary and footnotes. But a year later, when Schneider again complained that a Google search of his name still directed users to us, I made sure that the pages in the search engine's archive were updated.

Schneider was wrongly blamed, and to my knowledge he's the only person this has happened to in the entire history of WikiLeaks. Personally, I felt sorry for him. But all the other complaints, threats, and demands we received before and after ultimately proved to be attempts by people to conceal their own wrongdoing. People would Google themselves and see a link to WL. Outraged, they would then contact us, and no form of threat, demand, or attempt at bribery was too stupid for them to try out. It was fun messing around with them.

One good example was a set of leaks surrounding a complaint filed by Rudolf Elmer. Elmer was, up until 2003, Julius Bär's vice president on the Cayman Islands, but in 2008 he filed testimony with the European Court of Justice about various human rights violations. (As was reported shortly before this book went to press, Elmer was the source behind the Julius Bär leaks.) In part of one sentence in his complaint, he wrote that a certain John Reilley* had consulted with the bank about how he could avoid paying taxes. Asking for such a consultation alone is a crime. Reilley is a well-known investor, whose homepage celebrates him as a major financer of social projects and a "philanthropist." A good guy, you'd think.

A couple of days after we published Elmer's letter of complaint, a man named Richard Cohen* contacted us. He began by heaping praise upon WikiLeaks and ended up offering to make a donation. PayPal wasn't working, so he suggested organizing a fund-raising event for us in Manhattan. In a seemingly off-the-cuff remark, he mentioned that he had "accidentally" searched for his broker's name on the WL site, and lo and behold, there was John Reilley, mentioned in connection with tax evasion. But Reilley's integrity was beyond doubt, he said. Perhaps this was a result of a mistake in our translation?

His tone got a lot less friendly when we wrote back briefly, saying that our translation was perfectly fine and the case was, as far as we were concerned, closed. He threatened with attorneys, lawsuits, and other legal measures. He said he was going to inform everyone from Transparency International to God himself. For more than a page, Cohen went on about how we were going to get blown out of the sky, crushed like an insect, and scraped from the bottom of his boot. Our next answer was even more succinct: "Stop wasting our time and yours with this idiocy."

I admit I enjoyed imagining our adversaries chewing up the leather on their armchairs in rage. It wasn't as if a few people in this life hadn't gotten my own blood boiling.

We began developing a sixth sense for the true agendas behind such requests. E-mails that began by singing our praises were highly suspicious. They always ended badly when we failed to do as the sender had asked. Our response was to publish the e-mails with all the hymns and curses on our page. That was the best way of putting an immediate end to the tirades.

Publishing everything we received was part of our concept of transparency. What else could we do if we didn't want to open ourselves up to accusations of playing favorites? Whether the material affected the political right or the left, the good guys or the idiots, we published it. We only filtered out what was irrelevant. Admittedly, some of our publications went pretty far, containing private e-mails that carried implications for the lives of uninvolved third parties. One leak we published, for example, was the e-mail correspondence of the notorious Holocaust denier David Irving. In doing so, we indirectly ruined a reading tour he was planning for the United States. Once the places he was scheduled to appear became public knowledge, none of the organizers wanted to deal with protests by Irving's detractors. On the other hand, the e-mails also revealed the bullying way the controversial historian treated his own assistant. One would imagine that this was unpleasant for the woman in question. Who enjoys being revealed as a bully's victim? But in order to remain impartial, our desire for transparency had to become an ironclad principle. Otherwise, we could have been accused of being subjective or emotional in our choice of what to publish.

For Julian in particular, principles were more important than anything else. When one of our sources discovered a misconfiguration on the website of Senator Norm Coleman of Minnesota and sent us the publicly visible data, Julian wanted to publish not only the names of Coleman's campaign supporters but their exact credit card details, including security codes, as well. We sent out e-mails to all the people concerned, telling them to block their accounts. (Their data had been going around the Internet exchange forums for a couple of weeks anyway.) But I thought the risks were too great and served no purpose. What was the point of knowing the exact account details of all of Coleman's contributors?

That was what *I* thought. After a lot of argument, we agreed to publish the data with the last digits of the credit card numbers blacked out. Julian seemed to delight in provoking people as much as possible. He was of the opinion that people liked to get upset. He thought, for instance, that spam was a welcome evil because it gave people an excuse to complain. You were doing them a favor by spamming them. As it happened, he had himself pressed the wrong button on our mailing list at one point so that 350,000 people received repeated e-mails with the message "At the moment, Julian Assange has no time for interviews." Our mailing address was put on a number of spam lists, and it wasn't easy to get off them. Nonetheless, Julian succeeded in putting a positive spin on the mishap by claiming that people were happy when you gave them the chance to get pissed off.

Another important rule of ours was to process documents in the order in which they had arrived. Our aim was to publish everything, as long as it had a modicum of relevance. We stuck by this principle until late 2009. By then, however, Julian in particular was demanding that we blow through the documents likely to attract the most media coverage first, and under extreme time pressure. This change in procedure was to cause considerable conflict between him and me. But back in the days of Julius Bär, the idea of us fighting was unthinkable. We rarely saw each other. Mostly we just chatted. But when we did meet up, he was very friendly. He always said "hoi" instead of hello and asked "How goes?" when he wanted to know how I was doing. Julian wasn't a particularly warm person, but he did have a talent for communicating a sense of mutual regard.

Often we were unable to meet in normal places. Julian worried about us being watched and thought it was dangerous for us to be seen together. I never picked him up from the airport or the train station. He would mostly just suddenly appear, knocking on my door late at night or telling me to go to some hastily arranged meeting point.

In the summer of 2008, after we hadn't seen each other in a long while, I picked him up at the Rosa-Luxemburg-Platz subway station in Berlin. He approached me, and we hugged.

"It's nice to see you," he said.

"I think so too," I answered.

I rarely meant those words more. It was simply great having

him around. Because I knew he was fighting for the same cause I was. Because I knew he cared as little as I did that we could have earned far more money selling our talents to businesses. Because I knew his aim too was to shake up society. To knock the bastards on the head, as he once put it.

We rented a car, a silver Mercedes C-Class station wagon, and packed the trunk full of small servers we had purchased with our first donations. Then we went on a whirlwind tour of Europe. This was long overdue. Our infrastructure was already straining under the growing levels of submissions and hits. In the beginning, it was all right just to pretend that we were bigger than we actually were. But our technical infrastructure was pretty much a joke. And irresponsible. If someone back then had found out where our server was located, he could have easily shut down WL permanently.

I had pieced together a map of locations both within and outside Germany—inconspicuous places that were nonetheless safe. The locations had to be kept top secret because, among other reasons, we didn't want the people who rented space for our servers to be put in danger.

We had a lot of driving ahead of us that weekend. By the time we returned the rental car twenty-four hours later, the employees at the drop-off would do a double take. There would be 2,100 additional kilometers on the odometer. I put the pedal to the metal, constantly monitoring the cars in my rearview mirror in case someone was shadowing our clandestine undertaking. Julian sat beside me, bitching. He was a terrible backseat driver. He complained the entire time that I was driving too fast, and to him as an Australian, the German roads seemed far too narrow and full of traffic. What's more, he never quite got over the feeling that I was driving on the wrong side of the road.

In one of the many computing centers where we installed our servers, Julian would casually grab a power cord from the room next door and cut it in two. After a bit of tinkering he had a new power source for his laptop—the power cord and adapter he had brought with him were never long enough to reach the nearest outlet. He wasn't bothered by the fact that computing centers usually have surveillance cameras, or that the employees there usually don't take kindly to people simply cutting through cables.

When we reached Switzerland, I spent all my remaining money on Ovaltine. I love the Swiss chocolate drink, and for the rest of our tour, I couldn't wait to get back home and make myself a huge cup of cocoa. But when we arrived back in Wiesbaden, the cocoa powder would be all gone. Julian had at some point torn open the packages and poured the contents straight into his mouth.

In Switzerland we briefly considered taking a photo of ourselves, posing as conquering heroes, in front of the Julius Bär building. If we'd had more time, we certainly would have. Bär is the German word for bear, and that became a running gag in our conversations. We no longer talked about David versus Goliath, but David versus the bears.

In the coming months, we would have more significant leaks in terms of their global political relevance—revelations that would earn spots on twenty-minute nightly national news broadcasts. But we never enjoyed any of our triumphs more than the victory we'd achieved over the bears. Julius Bär was a banking house with unlimited resources that had been represented by a powerful and aggressive law firm, and they had been powerless against us and our cleverly constructed system.

The alpha bears were no doubt accustomed to making others hold their tongues with a single takedown letter. But they burned their paws on us. That made us proud. After all, where would you expect to find the most powerful and devious people if not there, where sums in the billions were bandied about? These people were adept at finding loopholes to secure deals. But they never came up with a lever to move us. We were just two guys with an out-of-date, tiny server. For the first time, I realized that we could stand up to anyone in the world.

It would be an exaggeration to say that this inflated my ego. I didn't exactly suffer from an inferiority complex to begin with. But if you've just shot down and killed a horde of bears, you do walk through the world with a bit broader shoulders.

It wasn't far from my apartment to the lefty alternative mac-robiotic shop where I bought my groceries. The shop was called Hazelnut, and it was only two streets away. I didn't have much contact anymore with the nondigital world, and the shop was one of the few places I still interacted with people face-to-face. Whenever I entered the shop after our adventure with Julius Bär, I felt like saying, "If you knew who we just fucked over, you'd laugh."

The same three people always worked in the shop, and we'd chat sometimes while they packed the cream or *Schwedenmilch* I had just bought. At one point, they asked what I did for a living. I tried to tell them about the Internet and the fight against cor-ruption, but I think the only thing they got out of my attempts at an explanation was that I was one of those crazy IT lunatics.

They smiled as they put a jar of fair-trade peanut butter in my bag. "A free sample," they said. The conversation turned to sandwich spreads. They were more interested in that than in me. Two years later, when I was back in Wiesbaden visiting my parents, they recognized me. They had seen my face on TV.

But back to 2008. There were always newspapers lying about at Hazelnut—small publications that wrote about the world from a queer and/or Marxist perspective, not the big mainstream newspapers. A couple of them had run articles about the Julius Bär story. Sometimes I would glance over at the pile and laugh to myself. The employees at Hazelnut had no idea that one of those WikiLeaks people described in those articles was none other than the haggard, poorly shaven guy in printed T-shirts who bought his breakfast cream from them every day.

3

The Scientology Handbooks

THERE wasn't time for us to rest on our laurels. A short while after the Julius Bär leaks, we received the first documents concerning Scientology. We didn't know where they had come from. But it could hardly have been a coincidence that around the same time, a host of "Anonymous" users began chatting on our site.

Anonymous was an international group of Net activists who had declared war on Scientology. They owed their name to the fact that Internet users who want to participate in forums or image boards without revealing their identities are always given "Anonymous" as a user name. The members of the group could be recognized by the Guy Fawkes mask they have borrowed from the graphic novel *V for Vendetta*. Guy Fawkes was an English revolutionary who tried to blow up the British Parliament in 1605, and the protagonists in *V for Vendetta* wore masks with a likeness of his face. Members of Anonymous also used Guy Fawkes masks whenever they appeared in YouTube videos or public acts of protest.

The masks with their pointy beards and horrifically frozen

grins are somewhat unsettling. The German Anonymous website, though, explained that the disguises were inspired by their own fear of their enemy, Scientology:

> It might appear as though we are trying to frighten people, but we aren't. Scientology has no qualms about persecuting ordinary citizens who protest against their machinations. What we mean by persecute is shadowing and harassing individuals just because they do not share Scientology's view of the world. We are only protecting ourselves against intimidation and harassment. The Scientology organization is incredibly wealthy. It has an unbelievable team of lawyers at its disposal and is known for its nuisance lawsuits. That's the reason for the masks.

Anonymous signs all its videos and messages with the slogan "Knowledge is free. We are Anonymous. We are Legion. We do not forgive. We do not forget. Expect us!"

Scientology was a powerful adversary. The sect had been able to muzzle a lot of people who wanted to reveal its secrets. Former members, in particular, who had broken with Scientology and wanted to warn others about the sect's methods were flooded with lawsuits, harassed, and intimidated.

With WikiLeaks, insiders had the chance to publish their information without the risk of Scientology figuring out who they were and suing them. The Julius Bär leaks had proven that there was nothing you could do to stop us.

To start with, we concentrated on publishing the sect's handbooks. We had penetrated the "system" bank. Now we were immersing ourselves in the "system" sect. I'd never paid much attention to Scientology before that. And I was riveted.

As a Scientologist, one works, so to speak, one's way up the career ladder, level by level, with the goal of becoming "clear." Depending on how one performs, one achieves a certain "Thetan level" in the process. At each level, members are required to pay a hefty fee for the training they receive.

Thetans are curious creatures. The story goes that millions of years ago our solar system, which consisted of seventy-six planets, was suffering from overpopulation. An intergalactic warrior named Xenu traveled throughout the galaxies on a mission to save the day. Like a mirror image of the biblical Noah, Xenu gathered up the scum of the universe's population—above all, criminals and other dubious characters. He then had them killed here on Earth by putting them all inside a Hawaiian volcano and detonating a hydrogen bomb. What could be more logical!

Ever since, Thetans have wandered the Earth as spirits in search of primitive people whose bodies they can attach themselves to in order to regain material form. If someone has a problem, it's because of the Thetan still dwelling deep within him. That's the basic teaching of Scientology, which claims to help people free themselves from their inner Thetans. The sect's founder, L. Ron Hubbard, claimed in radio broadcasts from the 1950s, which we also published, that he was several hundred million years old and that he was traveling the galaxy to observe things.

Probably because it is felt that such nonsense would be too much for new members, the sect only imparts this information when members have reached a certain point on the career ladder. Before that, they are under no circumstances allowed to take even a peek at that part of the "holy scriptures." Scientologists only learn as of level 5, for instance, that their world is populated by aliens.

The handbooks are not only secret, they're expensive. In order to be clued in about the existence of aliens, for example, a member usually has to have reached a level requiring a cumulative payment of fees to Scientology equivalent to the cost of a single-family home. In this perverse sense, the books that we published on our site were worth at least hundreds of thousands of dollars.

According to Scientology, those who don't overcome their Thetans quickly enough have to be "rehabilitated." If someone is particularly unlucky, he lands in a so-called Rehabilitation Force Project (RFP). This is like a Scientology juvenile detention center. Scientology also runs a fleet of ships consisting of cruise liners. The sect's private navy is called Sea Organization, or Sea Org for short. Anyone who fails to live up to expectations on these ships can be sent to the RFP unit. There a member may undergo a series of absurd punishments. For example, a member may be forced to wear a black rubber full-body suit and be isolated from the rest of the crew. He may be allowed to eat only after everyone else is through with their meals, and get only the scraps left behind by his fellow members. He's not allowed to sleep for more than seven hours. He may not be allowed to move at a normal pace, but rather be forced to run around. In particularly bad cases, he would be forced to run around in circles on deck, no matter how hot it gets in the rubber suit.

He may have to empty the latrines onboard or carry out like-wise degrading tasks that other members can assign to him at any time. He may be allowed to resume other activities—for instance, his own spiritual development—once he has carried out his punitive assignments.

In 1995, a young woman named Lisa McPherson died while under the sway of Scientology. Her death unleashed the first significant wave of outrage against the sect, which until then had been relatively unknown.

The circumstances surrounding McPherson's death have never been fully determined. What's known is that the thirty-six-year-old was brought to a hospital after suffering a nervous breakdown following a minor traffic accident. There she was picked up by two Scientologists who said they had documents proving they were responsible for McPherson's well-being.

The woman was subjected to a so-called Introspection Rundown in one of the rehabilitation units. We were the first people ever to publish the concrete procedures for this, as laid out by Scientology. According to those procedures, people undergoing an Introspection Rundown aren't allowed to speak with anyone. Isolation is supposed to teach them to free themselves from their situation. But for a person suffering a psychological crisis, isolation can be fatal. This was the case with Lisa McPherson. The coroner also determined she had been given far too little to drink. Dehydration and being confined to bed led to a thrombosis that went undetected or untreated. McPherson died of a respiratory embolism. Her "rundown" ended in her death. Scientologists handed over her body, which was in very poor condition, to a hospital in Florida on December 5, 1995.

The authorities subsequently began investigating Scientology leaders for failing to offer needed medical help and practicing medicine without a doctor's license. But the charges were dropped when the medical examiner ultimately determined that her death was accidental. In 2004, in a civil trial, McPherson's next of kin agreed to a settlement with Scientology. The deal remains undisclosed.

Among other things, what made our Scientology leak so valuable was that it contained the precise procedure for a "rundown." We also collected a number of internal audio and video recordings and published lists of companies and agencies that had connections to the Scientology network. On those lists were companies that ran hiring tests for other firms and for social-service organizations—among them, one responsible for combating drug addiction in the United States.

The members of Anonymous were a great help to us in structuring this material. They organized and sorted the way we presented it on the Internet and provided a lot of useful information. I spoke to some of them on the telephone. I was always running to call shops in the middle of the night to phone American or British numbers. I would stand in a call box, leaning against the wood-chip wall, surrounded by the comforting chatter in German of Arab, Indian, or African exiles, and listen to horror stories from the lives of ex-Scientologists. Sometimes these calls went into the wee hours of the morning.

To stay awake, I'd buy a bottle of Club-Mate, a soft drink containing stimulants. I kept it beside the phone as I tried to calm down the unknown individual on the other end of the line. One of them said he feared for his life after leaving Sea Org. The next one wanted to know how he could get us video material. Others just wanted to talk. Actually, all of them wanted to talk. In particular, those ex-Scientologists who had only recently left the sect were usually at their wit's end and were thankful that a young German took the time to listen to them. At least with me they had the impression that contacting someone wasn't going to put them at risk. I was a pro when it came to questions of security.

The call-shop employees were no doubt used to dubious-looking characters who wanted to make their calls with complete anonymity. But I was an especially frequent customer. I probably still have around a hundred SIM cards lying around at home, stored in film containers. Most practical for my purposes were the preregistered cards that are widely available under the counter. Sometimes, I'd buy a whole series of numbers, search the Web for the names and addresses of large families (birthday party announcements on blogs were a good source), and then register the cards to those people. There was no way anyone could tell who was calling whom.

Transferring documents was also secure. We took care that controversial documents were sent through so many detours, encryptions, and anonymizing procedures, and were accompanied by such a large amount of white noise as a diversion, that no one could trace where they came from. We were likewise unable to contact our sources, even in cases when clarifications were urgently necessary. The sender left no traces on the Web, not even the smallest fingerprint or data fragment. Nothing.

The informants did not have to fear any lawsuits. We, on the other hand, hoped that Scientology would try to sue *us*. The sect would almost surely have lost any suit it chose to file, and the case would have attracted more public interest in the spectacular documents, as had been the case with Julius Bär. At the time, there were monthly anti-Scientology protests in almost every major city. Members of Anonymous, for instance, had held up signs at one such protest saying SUE WL, YOU FAGGOTS!

But the leaders of the sect were either cleverer than our adversaries at the bank or lucky enough to come after them. The case of Julius Bär had shown the whole world that one could only lose by suing us.

Personally, I was most fascinated by the cult of personality surrounding Scientology's founder, L. Ron Hubbard. In older recordings, he was shown or heard holding talks at universities in which he told his audience that he was millions of years old and was traveling from planet to planet to check that everything was OK. At first people laughed. But by the end of any given broadcast, you sensed that an almost friendly relationship had built up between Hubbard and the listeners in the auditorium. Hubbard had a special talent. He was a captivating storyteller, knew how to laugh at himself, and could serve up even the most absurd stories with a straight face.

During this period, Julian and I used to joke about whether it would make sense for us to found a religion. It would have solved a lot of problems. If, for example, not enough people were reading the documents we thought were important, we could have sent out a team like the Jehovah's Witnesses. They could have rung people's doorbells and read our leaks out loud: "Are you aware of the paragraph about your local water utility—millions in cor-ruption!" It is ironic that Facebook today includes a page for a religion called Assangism!

The guys from Anonymous helped us present the Scientol-ogy leaks. They prepared the site so that readers could find their way more easily through the deluge of documents. They were all volunteers.

We could have benefited from something similar for lots of other material, but in general it was hard to motivate outsiders to work with us. It was becoming increasingly clear that we were not going to be able to handle everything ourselves. New people were constantly getting in touch via the chat room and offering to help. But how could we know that they stood for the same ideals we did? And that they wouldn't let important security information slip?

An all-consuming religion would have simplified a lot of things. Those who worked for Scientology were highly motivated, despite the sometimes hair-raising conditions in which they lived and worked. Scientology took everything they had to give, and when their money ran out, people would mortgage their houses and sell off their belongings. Or they could do work for Scientol-ogy. In return, they received neither a pension nor a vacation—members sometimes even signed over their insurance policies to the sect.

Looking back, I ask myself whether WikiLeaks itself has devel-oped into a kind of religious cult. It's become a system that admits little internal criticism. Anything that went wrong had to be the fault of something on the outside. The guru was beyond ques-tion. The danger had to be external. This mind-set encouraged internal cohesion. Anyone who offered too much criticism was punished by having his rights suspended or by being threatened with possible consequences. Moreover, WL participants were only allowed to know as much as was absolutely necessary for them to carry out their appointed tasks.

In any case, this much can be said: From reading the Scientology documents, and the philosophy and teachings of L. Ron Hubbard, Julian learned only too well how a cult of personality functions.

4

Dealing with
the Media

OUR work brought us in contact with cults, clandestine operations, judicial trickery, and marketing strategies, and we learned a lot from the people we were fighting against. Later, when it came to our own finances, Julian would try to avail himself of concealment tactics similar to those used by Julius Bär. Like Scientology, we didn't want outsiders to be able to see our internal structures, and we encouraged a sense of mystery concerning who was who on our team. In late 2010, while being pursued by Swedish prosecutors, Julian would apply for asylum in Switzerland, the very country we had sought to nail for its banking secrecy laws and cowardly politicians.

The next terrain in which we were forced to find our feet was the press landscape. From the media we tried to learn how to manipulate public opinion.

At this point, we'd had some experience with the newspapers and broadcasters—and not all of it was good. One important lesson we learned was that in cases of crisis, it was better to divert people's attention than to waste energy trying to deny one's own shortcomings and mistakes or to argue them out of existence. The latter was far too time-consuming! At first, I would cheerfully provide information on every little mishap, but the public has a short memory. All that counted was the next story. When there was something new to write about, no one asked anymore about old problems.

One day a journalist from a left-wing newspaper in Berlin asked whether our IT and legal system in Sweden really would stand up to a serious test. It, after all, was the basis of assurances of protection we gave to our sources. In fact, there was a chink in our security that we had overlooked. The journalist wasn't the only one to suggest that our system was anything but impregnable.

When I approached Julian, he didn't want to hear anything about the problem.

"The author is misinformed," he snapped.

Julian thought the majority of journalists were idiots. A short time later, he sent the following tweet: "The article currently being spun about WikiLeaks source protection is false."

For him, that was the end of the matter. The strategy worked. To create the impression of unassailability to the outside world, you only had to make the context as complicated and confusing as possible. To that end, I would make my explanations of technical issues to journalists as complex as I could. It was the same principle used by terrorists and bureaucrats. The adversary can't attack as long as he has nothing to grab hold of. Modern-day customer relations works in a similar way. A customer who wants to complain but can never find anyone responsible to talk to ultimately has no choice but to swallow his anger.

For us, the important thing was not how something really was, but how one sold it. Addressing a problem, to say nothing of taking a public stance toward it, would have meant making it a reality. For a long time, Julian had great success with his strategy of ignoring problems until they disappeared. In retrospect, it's amazing how long this strategy worked.

Over the course of time, we also learned which journalists to work with to ensure that our news attracted maximum attention. When in doubt, we prioritized newspapers or programs that could guarantee us a larger and more varied audience over those that were better informed and asked cleverer questions but were only read by people who were on our side to begin with.

However, our interest in working with the largest mass media organs also had limits, as the case of Toll Collect was to prove. In late 2009, we published more than 10,000 pages of secret contracts between the German government and Daimler-Benz, Deutsche Telekom, and the French highway company Cofiroute—a joint venture called Toll Collect. In return for setting up an electronic toll system on Germany's autobahn, the German government had guaranteed Toll Collect a utopian return of 19 percent. The sum in question was more than a billion euros, and there was no way revenues were going to live up to German government assurances. Taxpayers would inevitably be left footing the bill. Everyone involved agreed that the content of those contracts should not be made public.

We decided to provide our material exclusively to two journalists, who would then analyze and summarize it. In our experience, complicated leaks—and the Toll Collect contract material was enormously complicated—had to be published by the traditional media in digestible chunks. No matter how explosive our revelations were, if no one presented them to the general public, they would languish, neglected, on our website. As partners we chose the IT journalist Detlef Borchers, who had already written a lot about the topic for a German publisher specializing in computing issues, and Hans-Martin Tillack, a reporter for the weekly magazine *Stern* and an experienced, prizewinning journalist. We hoped that working with *Stern* would allow us to reach the broadest possible audience. The magazine had more than seven million readers and was available at hair salons and in doctors' offices throughout Germany.

I met Tillack at his office at Berlin's Hackescher Markt. The office was on the seventh or eighth floor, and from his windows there was a good view of this busy shopping and business square in the heart of the German capital. Tillack was sitting in front of his imposing bookshelves, his hands folded in front of his stomach. He was an impatient man of forty-nine who was fully absorbed in his role as the experienced star journalist. "Yeah, yeah," he would often interject before I had the chance to finish my sentences. Still, while he may have treated me like a schoolboy, I could see the glimmer in his eyes the first time I took a copy of the Toll Collect contracts from my bag. Tillack assured me that WikiLeaks would have a prominent place in his article.

"I'm convinced we'll find a solution for how to properly acknowledge WL so that you'll be satisfied," he wrote me after our meeting.

It was important to me for him to explain how WikiLeaks functioned as a platform and what the project was about. But when I called him later to ask whether he needed any additional information from me, he got irritated and I became concerned that WikiLeaks might not get a sufficient credit.

Ultimately, the article he wrote was a great disappointment, as he implied that the story was primarily based on his own investigative research. There was no background information about WikiLeaks. We only came in for a mention late in the main body of the article:

> The contract material was transmitted to the proprietors
> of the website WikiLeaks, which specializes in secret
> documents and which plans to put the contracts online
> in their entirety.

I tried to stay calm. What was I getting so upset about? We'd simply never work with Tillack again. The response he sent me after my first complaint about the article spoke volumes:

> It was the maximum I could get. My bosses asked me
> why we had [to] mention WikiLeaks at all. And since
> the documents in this case had dimensions far beyond
> some pharmaceutical company, you didn't just get
> mentioned in *WirtschaftsWoche,* but in *Stern,* which
> has a circulation of one million and readership of seven
> million!
>
> Regards, Hans-Martin Tillack

However, we also had lots of good experiences with the media. The business newspaper *WirtschaftsWoche,* for instance, honored all their agreements, and so did *Zeit Online* when we gave them the field report about the bombing of two hijacked tanker trucks in Kunduz a couple of hours before we posted them on WL. At the time, the report about possible mistakes by German colonel Georg Klein was already in the possession of a handful of well-connected German newspapers and magazines. But instead of making all the information available to the general public, they had smugly chosen to cite only small snippets. *Zeit Online* wrote about the report comprehensively and directed readers to the full version of it on WL so they could make up their minds for themselves.

This was the role we were often to play in the future. We made source documents, from which the media cited only excerpts, available in their entirety. Other media either lacked the proper platforms to do this themselves or they feared legal consequences, or, what was probably more often the case, individual journalists simply did not want to share exclusive material with their colleagues.

We were forced to learn which topics would make a splash in the media and which would attract less interest. The two-page *Stern* article on Toll Collect, for instance, had been followed by a much-longer, meandering report about alternative religion and was most notable for its illustrations: photos of naked women smoking cigars.

We had to accept that the most significant leaks were not always the ones that attracted public attention. What captivated people's imaginations were leaks that could be easily understood and discussed by the masses. People were immensely interested, for example, in Sarah Palin's hacked e-mail account. What was leaked there was hardly scandalous. At the most, Palin could have been criticized for having used her private account to send internal party messages. Her account also contained a family portrait and some private photos of her children. But the media never tired of talking over the leak.

I thought the leak of Palin's hacked e-mail was weak and of questionable relevance. But releasing the material was in keeping with our philosophy of publishing all documents uncensored. It was also part of our larger strategy. With every leak, we tried to extend the frontiers of what we could do into previously unknown terrain. Then we would push ahead in the same direction with our next leak.

What is public, and what is private? We were trying to stir up controversy about this very question. And it was better for the debate to center on Sarah Palin's e-mail account than on the data of private consumers. We were convinced that we were strengthening the project by pushing the limits of what was acceptable, and getting our way in the end. We became increasingly brazen. No one could shut us down.

In comparison with the stir caused by Palin's e-mail account, the public didn't take much interest in the files we published in November 2009 concerning a German pharmaceutical company. If I had to name my favorite leaks from that year, these files would definitely be among them. They read like a case study in corruption and can be easily understood by laymen.

The files concerned payments made by pharmaceutical representatives to doctors so that they would prescribe more of the company's medications. We published ninety-six pages of investigations carried out by police and prosecutors. They detailed the practices used by some pharmaceutical company representatives.

If doctors prescribed their patients those products, they received a cut of the additional profits. Moreover, there were direct payments. In an internal e-mail, one of the company's regional directors had written, "If a doctor wants money, call me and we'll find a way." Another means of encouraging physicians to prescribe more of the company's products was to give them coupons for expensive seminars.

But because an internal judicial inquiry had concluded that licensed doctors could not be charged with corruption in this case, the investigations had largely been suspended by the time of the leak. Public interest in the files was scant.

I also recall an interesting encounter I had on a program with a woman named Katrin Bauerfeind. She had begun her career with a German Internet program and had moved on to host a show of her own on the German-Swiss-Austrian network 3sat. I was invited as a guest on the program and drove to Cologne for the interview. When taping was over, her editor said she was struck by how optimistic I was and how much I believed other people were capable of.

I do indeed have a basically positive view of human nature. I think that people have an innate interest in being informed but are kept in a state of ignorance by the media, the politicians, and their bosses. If you provide people sufficient background information, they are capable of behaving correctly and making the right decisions, I told the editor.

Things were very different in her experience, she replied. She didn't think people were interested in complex issues. When I watched the show afterward, I had to ponder the age-old question of the chicken and the egg. The program was thirty minutes long, of which ten were devoted to me. The other parts of the show were titled things like "The Wall Fell and Berlin Dances to Techno" and "Miss Platinum—The Real Lady Gaga." I'm not saying the world would be a better place if they had spent all thirty minutes reporting on WL. But the show did make me ask which came first: bad programming or a bad audience. Perhaps all one had to do was put the audience back in a position to demand better programming.

Other leaks attracted little immediate interest but went on to inspire long-term analyses and scientific publications in expert journals. One example was our publication of all the text messages sent on September 11, 2001, before, during, and after the attacks on the World Trade Center. Researchers examined the messages, searching for key terms indicating sadness, fear, and anger. They concluded that the predominant emotion was anger and that, compared to words like sadness or fear, expressions of aggression increased in the days following the terrorist attacks.

Others were interested in our publications about the Human Terrain System, which entails anthropologists helping the US military to adapt their propaganda to specific countries and cultures and steer relations with local populaces. The academic world was also fascinated by the Congressional Research Service, or CRS, reports. The American Congress has its own scientific intelligence service, which any congressman can use to obtain information.

The reports issued by the service are painstaking and high-quality, covering topics from the cotton industry in Mexico to weapons of mass destruction in China. Scientists would love to have access to these reports, which are paid for with taxpayer money. But the congressmen themselves decide on whether a given report gets published or not. Most of the time, they refuse permission.

The reasons vary. One is that the reports show when a particular congressman knew about a specific topic and make his interests in general transparent. In other cases, the reports don't yield the results a congressman would have liked. There was a similar case in Germany with a government study on private health insurance. When the researchers came to the conclusion that private insurers did not yield the sort of social benefits that had always been propagated, Germany's economics minister, Rainer Brüderle, who had commissioned the study, simply had it filed away under lock and key. In exactly the same sense, if published, a CRS report can show that legislation sponsored by a congressman is misguided, or that his positions are wrong and his administrative activities poorly organized. In any case, the reports had long occupied the top spot on the most wanted list of the Center for Democracy and Technology (CDT), a prominent American civil-rights organization specializing in technology and politics.

We posted thousands of CRS reports on our page. In terms of the tax money that went into producing them, they were worth more than a billion dollars. Demand was correspondingly high.

After a bit of time, we used Google to check where the reports had ended up. We found them, among other places, on government servers. That was an ironic triumph, and the open-data movement, which was becoming increasingly recognized at the time, was delighted. It's interesting to note that Senator John McCain had also demanded that the reports be published during his presidential campaign. McCain was a far more vigorous proponent of open government data than Barack Obama, even if Obama got more credit for his open government initiatives.

At the time, we considered whether to put a watermark on our documents to prevent journalists from using our material without referencing us. Quite often, stories would suddenly appear in the media without WL being named as a source just after we had published similar leaks. Whenever I inquired, I was usually told that the journalists in question had "gotten the material from someone else" or "had been holding it back for quite some time." If we had put watermarks on our documents, it would have been easier to catch the journalists. A request from an original document would have revealed whether someone was using our source. But watermarks would have been too difficult technically.

Without question, people could have accused us of demanding the sort of intellectual property protection that we ourselves criticized in other areas. I myself often wear T-shirts with the Pirate Bay logo and support progressive concepts of copyright. But there was more to our considerations than pure copyright interests. In some cases, we were concerned about being able to supplement documents with vital additional information or to prevent media sources from linking to documents that create false impressions if read without commentary. That was why we wrote summaries and occasionally offered judgments about the quality of our material.

A good example of what could happen with directly linked documents was the leak of the Memorandum of Understanding.

This was an agreement reached between the Kenyan politician Raila Odinga and Kenya's National Muslim Leaders Forum, which concluded with the approving knowledge of then presidential candidate Obama. Among other things, the agreement had the moderate Christian Odinga making concessions to Kenya's Muslim minority, including the promise to represent the interests of Muslim Kenyans detained at Guantánamo Bay.

Two documents, a genuine one and a fake one, were contained in the memorandum. The fake one suggested that Obama supported the introduction of Sharia law in Kenya, which was absurd. It was interesting to see which publications linked to which document, since one was clearly aimed at portraying Obama as a covert African Muslim and thereby depicting him as unfit to become president of the American people. The fake appeared in the *New York Sun* and various publications of the far right. All that the other document revealed was that Obama knew about the memorandum. If the documents had only existed as a complete package with watermarks and commentary, we would have been able to stop others in the media from using them to manipulate public opinion.

In December 2008, we were once again attending the Chaos Communication Congress. Unlike the previous year, Julian's lecture at the CCC was part of the official program, and it was very well attended. This time, Julian and I sat together onstage, and we'd risen in the world from the tiny space in the cellar. Indeed, our ascent had been meteoric, which of course meant a larger audience. Nine hundred people, and not just twenty, now wanted to hear Julian speak. More than once, a cracking voice came across the hall loudspeakers, asking people to please not block the emergency exits.

The requests were in vain. People were crowding the stairs and the hallway leading to the conference room. I found myself asking whether anyone except me noticed that Julian was wearing exactly the same clothes as the year before: a white shirt and olive-green cargo pants. But that was nonsense. None of the people now in attendance could have remembered us.

We got a few laughs when we read an e-mail of complaint we had received a few days previously from the German Intelligence Service, the Bundesnachrichtendienst, or BND. The head of the BND, Ernst Uhrlau, had gotten in touch personally—something he later denied, since it was quite unprofessional. The e-mail was written in German. It read [translated]:

> **To:** WikiLeaks@jabber.se
> **From:** Directorial Staff IVBB-BND-BIZ/BIZDOM
> **Date:** Tue, Dec 16, 2008 1:15 P.M.
> **Subject:** WG: Classified Report of the
> Bundesnachrichtendienst
>
> ---
>
> Dear Sir or Madam:
>
> On your homepage you enable the download of a classified report of the Bundesnachrichtendienst. I hereby demand that you immediately block this ability. I have already ordered a review of possible criminal consequences.
>
> Sincerely,
> Ernst Uhrlau
> President, Bundesnachrichtendienst

We responded in English:

> **From:** Sunshine Press Legal Office
>   <wl-legal@sunshinepress.org>
> **To:**   leitungsstab@bnd.bund.de
> **Cc:**   wl-office@sunshinepress.org,
>   wl-press@sunshinepress.org,
>   wl-germany@sunshinepress.org
> **Date:** Thu, Dec 18, 2008 9:35 A.M.
> **Subject:** Re: WG: Classified Report of the
>   Bundesnachrichtendienst
>
> ═══════════════════════════════════
>
> Dear Mr. Uhrlau,
>
> We have several BND-related reports. Could you be more precise?
>
> Thank you.
> Jay Lim

An answer, this time also in English, was quick to come:

> **To:**   Sunshine Press Legal Office
>   <wl-legal@sunshinepress.org>
> **Date:** Thu, Dec 18, 2008 5:59 P.M.
> **Subject:** Antwort: Re: WG: Classified Report of the
>   Bundesnachrichtendienst
>
> ═══════════════════════════════════
>
> Dear Mr. Lim,
>
> As of today you still provide the option of downloading a classified report of the BND under the following address: http://www.WikiLeaks.com/wiki/BND_Kosovo_intelligence-report,_22_Feb_2005.
>
> We kindly ask you again to remove the file immediately and all other files or reports related to the BND as

> well. Otherwise we will press for immediate criminal
> prosecution.
>
> Yours sincerely,
> Ernst Uhrlau
> President of the Bundesnachrichtendienst

Messages like this were a great way of showing that a document was genuine. Whenever someone demanded that we remove a document as quickly as possible, we always asked, under the pretense of a friendly request for clarification, whether the person who complained could prove he held the copyright to the material in question. Some of the people we dealt with were nice enough to provide us with a screenshot as evidence of ownership. We would then post that screenshot as well, secretly grateful that our adversaries were doing our job for us.

The leak in question concerned the BND's involvement in fighting criminality in Kosovo and its cooperation with journalists. Someone had sent us an internal paper from the German telecommunications giant Deutsche Telekom, listing two dozen secret IP addresses used by the BND to surf the Internet. We played a little game with them. Using the WikiScanner, one can trace what changes have been made to Wikipedia entries from any given IP address. Employees of the BND had made changes to the entries about military aircraft, nuclear weapons, and the BND itself.

Even more amusing were the "corrections" made to the entry on the Goethe Institute, the German government's premier institution for promoting German language and culture around the world. Originally the entry had stated that many Goethe Institute offices were used as unofficial points of contact by the BND. BND employees had altered it to say the exact opposite: "Foreign branches of the Goethe Institute are not used as unofficial homes for the BND." The entire sentence was later deleted from the entry.

In addition, according to the IP addresses, the BND had also been in contact with a Berlin escort service. Had this been to set a trap using a femme fatale, as in the good old days of the Cold War? Or had someone at the BND been feeling lonely and ordered the women for himself?

There were a couple of glitches in Julian's lecture at the congress. Every time he grabbed hold of the microphone, he yanked out the video connection from the computer so that the screen went blank. But such bumbling only made us all the more sympathetic to our audience.

After the lectures, I usually retreated to a sofa in the lounge to relax and watch the people flowing past. Julian tirelessly worked the other rooms in the Berliner Congress Center, always hoping to be discovered and approached.

5

Julian Assange

A FTER the CCC conference at the end of 2008, Julian came to Wiesbaden and lived with me for two months. This was typical of him. He didn't have a fixed address, crashing instead at other people's places. Usually, all he carried with him was his backpack with his two notebook computers and a bunch of cell-phone chargers—although he could seldom find the one he needed. He wore several layers of clothing. Even indoors, he wore two pairs of pants—though I've never understood why—and even several pairs of socks.

In Berlin we had caught the "conference plague." That's what club members call the flu that spreads at this time of year when large numbers of people gather, breathe in the same conference air, and share the same keyboards. Ashen-faced, silent, and sick, we sped back to Wiesbaden in an overcrowded high-speed train on January 1, 2009. No sooner had we gotten back to my apartment, than the flu forced us to take to our beds. Or to be more precise, since I was feeling a bit better, I let Julian have my bed and withdrew to a mattress.

Julian pulled on all the clothes he could find and even fished some ski pants out of his backpack. Dressed like this, he went to bed, wrapped himself in two more woolen blankets of mine, and sweated out his fever. He was healthy again when he got up two days later. An efficient solution to the problem.

I lived in the Westend district of Wiesbaden. It's quite a rough part of the city, an area where it's wise to chain up your bike with an extra-heavy lock. The district had the advantage of having more cell-phone shops than supermarkets, and it was easy to purchase cheap handsets and cards.

My apartment was a basement walk-down that faced out to the road. At first the fact that people could look into my apartment made Julian pretty nervous. We pulled down the blind—a transparent, yellow paper thing with a Tibetan flag I had pinned in the middle. It let through a fuzzy warm light. You might call it secondhand sunlight. I liked it.

After getting over our bout of flu, we worked alongside each other peacefully and diligently. We would sit in my living room, typing away at our laptops. I worked at the desk in the corner by the window, while Julian was ensconced in front of me on the sofa with his computer on his lap. He usually wore his olive-green down jacket with the hood pulled up and a blanket wrapped around his legs. I was a bit worried about my sofa. He had turned the lovely brown velour Rolf Benz couch, which my parents had been intending to throw out and I had rescued from ending up on the garbage heap, into his preserve. Julian ate everything with his hands, and he always wiped his fingers on his pants. I have never seen pants as greasy as his in my whole life. The sofa had survived the last thirty years. It was older than I was. I was afraid that it would take Julian just a few weeks to ruin it completely.

Julian aspired to type completely blind. It was almost medita-
tive. When he replied to e-mails, for instance, he typed at a furious pace, moving through the various text fields without glancing
at the screen once. He filled out the individual fields in his mind's
eye and jumped from one dialog box to the next using shortcut
keys. The connections were infuriatingly slow because our communication with the outside world was encrypted and rendered
anonymous by a number of mechanisms, and because our e-mails
were sent via a remote computer rather than by our own laptops.
If you typed something, it would take ages for it to appear on
the screen. Julian was nevertheless determined to do work at double speed—with his eyes closed, you might say. He told me that
working without optical feedback was a form of perfection, a victory over time. He finished what he was doing long before his
computer did.

We were already getting a few donations to our PayPal account
and had gotten into the habit of sending out thank-you e-mails at
regular intervals. In the e-mails we showed our appreciation, telling our supporters how important their contributions were and
that they were investing in the freedom of information. We took
turns doing this job. This time it was Julian's turn to write the
e-mail and paste in the names of all our current donors.

So there he was, sitting on my sofa in the yellow light, wrapped
in two blankets, rhythmically click-clacking away next to me,
writing his e-mails. But the aria came to an abrupt halt with a
quiet "Goddamn!" Julian had made a mistake. Because we were
sending the e-mails to several recipients, he had to change the "to"
line into a "bcc" so that the recipients could not see the names
of the other donors. And there was precisely where Julian had

slipped up. He had already pressed the Send button—thanks to his perfect way of working.

This mistake bestowed on us our first and only homegrown leak in February 2009. The reaction to this thank-you e-mail did not take long in coming: "Please use the Blind Carbon Copy [bcc] to send e-mails of this kind" and "Unless you intended to leak the 106 e-mail addresses of your supporters, bcc would be better." One person offered us some remedial help: "If you don't know the difference, don't hesitate to contact me. I will be happy to guide you through the process."

Julian wrote an apology. Julian? No, "Jay Lim," our legal expert from the "WikiLeaks Donor Relations Department," the person in charge of donations.

As chance would have it, one of the donors whom we had thanked on this occasion was a certain Adrian Lamo. He was the semi-famous ex-hacker responsible for the arrest of US Army private Bradley Manning, who has been accused of being one of our sources.

"Look at that," Julian said when he discovered Lamo's contribution. "What an idiot!"

I clicked our mailbox and yes, there it was: a new secret document. Someone had sent us our own donor list as an official leak, along with a relatively unfriendly comment. Normally, we don't know who our sources are. But Lamo would later confess that he was the one who had confronted us with our own blunder. For good or for evil, we were going to have to reveal it.

It was interesting because we had spent some time philosophizing about what would happen if we were compelled to publish something about our own organization. We agreed that we had to release things that were bad as well as good publicity. In fact, our internal leak went down well with the press. At least we were consistent and none of the donors complained.

Julian often behaved as though he had been raised by wolves rather than by other human beings. Whenever I cooked, the food would not, for instance, end up being shared equally between us. What mattered was who was quicker off the mark. If there were four slices of SPAM, he would eat three and leave one for me if I was too slow. I wondered if I was being small-minded when things my mother used to say would pop into my mind occasionally. Things like "You could at least ask."

We both liked raw meat—steak tartare with onions. The fact that I took longer to eat my share was because I ate it with whole-grain bread and butter, while Julian preferred to eat his food without any accompaniments. He would eat meat or cheese or chocolate or bread. If he thought that citrus fruit would do him good, he would suck one lemon after another. And sometimes food would occur to him in the middle of the night after he hadn't consumed a single bite all day.

It was not that he had never learned any manners. Julian could be very polite when he wanted to. For example, he frequently accompanied my visitors—even when he didn't know them—out the door, into the lobby, and onto the street. It was as if he wanted to make sure that they were safe.

Julian was very paranoid. He was convinced that someone was watching my house, so he decided we should avoid ever being seen leaving or returning to the apartment together. I used to wonder what difference that made. If someone had gone to the trouble of shadowing my apartment, he would have seen us together anyway.

If we'd been in town together, Julian always insisted that we take separate routes home. He went the left way around while I went right. As a result, I often ended up waiting for him because he had gotten lost. I have never met anyone with such a bad sense of direction. Julian could walk into a telephone booth and forget which direction he had come from when he came out again. He regularly managed to walk past the door to my apartment building. You couldn't have behaved more conspicuously than Julian did. He used to walk up and down the street, looking left and right, trying to identify my front door, until at some point I came and collected him.

Perpetually concerned with finding a new look and the perfect disguise, he had borrowed a blue East German sweatshirt from me and teamed it with a brown baseball cap. I laughed to myself at his childlike urge to play. He didn't look any less conspicuous as a result, but his obvious disguise was somewhat touching. The next time that I went to look for him, he came around the corner dressed like this, with a wooden pallet on his shoulder. The pallet had come from a building site. I wasn't convinced that this was a very professional disguise.

Sometimes I think Julian had been overly influenced by certain books, which, mixed with his own imagination, had resulted in a special set of Julian Assange rules of conduct. This reminded me of Scientology founder L. Ron Hubbard, who had started off as a science-fiction writer and then began believing his own stories.

Julian, too, had a very free and easy relationship with the truth. I had the impression that he often tested out how far he could go. For example, he had served me up a story about how his hair had gone white. He told me that when he was fourteen, he had built a reactor at home in his basement and got the poles reversed. From that day on, his hair had grown in white as a result of the gamma radiation. Yeah, sure, I thought. I believe he wanted to see what he could get away with before I would say "Stop! I don't believe you." I thought that this was no way to treat other people. Mostly I said nothing.

Julian was constantly losing his way, getting onto the wrong train and walking in the wrong direction. Whenever he flew from A to B, or traveled by boat or train, a few receipts or documents would go astray. He was always waiting "really urgently" for a letter that would get him out of the next jam: the signature for an account, a new credit card, or a license for a contract. It was always beyond question that this letter would arrive by "tomorrow at the latest." If you asked him what had become of something that he had promised, he never said that he hadn't managed to get something done, or that something had slipped his mind, or that he had messed up. Instead he'd say, "I'm just waiting for John Doe or Joe Schmo to respond. He hasn't gotten back to me yet." If the admonition "Don't put off till tomorrow what you can do today" hadn't been around for ages, it would have been coined especially for Julian. Rarely was anything his fault. Instead he blamed banks, airport staff, urban planners, and, failing that, the State Department. No doubt it was the State Department that was responsible for dropping the cups that got broken while he was staying with me in Wiesbaden.

For all his flaws, Julian could concentrate in a way like no one else I've ever seen. He could commune with his computer screen for days on end, becoming one with it, forming a single, immovable entity. When I went to bed late, he'd often be sitting there like a thin Buddha on the sofa. When I woke up the next day, Julian would be sitting in a hooded sweatshirt in exactly the same position in front of the computer. Sometimes, when I went to bed the next night, he would still be sitting there.

You usually couldn't speak to him when he was working. He sat in deep meditation, programming or reading something or other. At most he used to leap up briefly without any warning and do some strange kung fu exercises. Some media reports said that Julian was at least the equivalent of a black belt in all known international martial arts. In fact, his improvised shadowboxing lasted a maximum of twenty seconds, looked extremely silly, and was probably intended to stretch his joints and tendons after all that sitting.

Julian could work for days on end and then suddenly fall asleep. He would lie down in all his pants, socks, and sweatshirts, pull the blanket over his head, and drop off. When he woke up, he snapped back into the world just as instantaneously. He would jump up, usually bumping into something. I had a dumbbell bench in the apartment, and I don't know how many times he leaped up from the mattress where he slept and rammed into the iron bars. There was always a huge crash-bang-wallop, and I would think, "Great. Julian has woken up."

One of his amusing quirks was his desire to wear clothes to match his current state of mind. Or perhaps he thought he could only get into the right mood by wearing the right clothes.

"Daniel, I need a jacket. Do you have one?" he would say.

"Do you want to go out?"

"I have to write a very important statement today."

"You what?"

Even though he usually sat at the kitchen table in hooded sweatshirt and cap, I suddenly had to lend him a jacket so that he could write a press release. He wouldn't take off the jacket the whole day, wearing a serious face the whole time he composed his text. Afterward, he would also go to bed in the jacket.

In the two months he lived with me, I got to know someone utterly unlike the guys I usually spent my time with. I was used to strong characters; that wasn't the point. On the one hand, I found Julian unbearable and, on the other, unbelievably special and lovable. I had the feeling that something must have gone very wrong in his life. He could have been a great person, and I was proud to have a friend who had such fire in his belly, who was so utterly committed to ideas and principles and changing the world for the better. Someone who just got up and did things without concern for what other people said. In certain respects I tried to copy this attitude. But he also had a dark side, and this increasingly gained the upper hand in the months to come.

Some friends asked me how I was able to put up with Julian for so long. I think that everyone has a difficult side. It is not easy to get along with anyone. In the hacker scene, in particular, there are quite a few extreme characters. Many seem slightly autistic. I'm probably more tolerant than most when it comes to others' eccentricities and quirks. That's why I put up with Julian for so long—probably longer than anyone else.

On February 17, 2009, I was invited to be a guest on the podcast program *Küchenradio*. Julian wrote the following e-mail to our supporters:

> Daniel Schmitt on Berlin's Keutchenradio [sic]: A two-
> hour video and audio interview session with our German
> correspondent, Daniel Schmitt, will be broadcast on
> Berlin's well-regarded Kuechenradio at 21:00 tonight.

Reading that today makes me gulp a bit. I had almost forgotten what a good time we had together. He wrote "well regarded"— *Küchenradio* is really a niche podcast for techies, but Julian was nonetheless proud of us. There are, of course, brief moments when I ask myself whether everything necessarily had to go sour. And whether we would still have been friends today if WikiLeaks hadn't been such a runaway success, if the money and the attention and the international pressure hadn't followed.

"Keutchenradio"—that was so Julian! He couldn't remember non-English words very well. He used to call *Der Spiegel* "The Speigel" even months after the German newsmagazine had become our closest media partner.

In the taxi on my way to see the journalist Philip Banse in the Neukölln district of Berlin, I received a phone call from my mother. My grandmother had died. We had been expecting the news any day. I hadn't even visited her one last time to say good-bye. I knew that my grandmother was proud of me and of my fight for a more just world. I felt ashamed that I hadn't been prepared to cancel my radio appearance to say good-bye to her properly. The rest of the family had spent the whole week at her bedside. But I had an appointment in Berlin, and that was more important to me.

At that point I felt like we had to take every opportunity to raise the profile of WikiLeaks. We were in desperate need of donations, and we were pleased when new documents were uploaded onto our site. Everything else came farther down on our list of priorities. Much farther down.

The first time that something Julian said really left a bitter taste in my mouth was in early 2009, when we were considering taking part in the World Social Forum in Brazil. A friend had mentioned to me that he would like to come with us. I told Julian about it. Personally, I was against the idea. This friend had nothing to do with the project, and we weren't going there on vacation, but rather to make contacts and to work. Not to mention the fact that I was paying for the tickets. Julian had no money.

Julian, on the other hand, thought it was an excellent idea and said, "Let him come along. He can carry our suitcases." When I looked incredulous, he said that he'd often done it in the past and that he liked having someone along to carry his bags. That was the first time I asked myself who was playing his porter right now. I couldn't think of anyone. Besides me.

I realized only later that Julian must have frequently interpreted my behavior as kowtowing. I just wanted to be friendly and considerate. I think that he must have regarded me as weaker than I actually was. Perhaps it's because I am an optimistic person who spends less time criticizing and more time getting things done. And our friendship began to fall apart the moment that Julian no longer felt that I was kowtowing to him. When I began to bring up concrete problems or criticize him, simply because problems existed and not because I saw our relationship differently, he started to describe me as someone who needed to be "contained."

In early 2010 his tone toward me changed radically. "If you fuck up, I'll hunt you down and kill you," he once told me. No one had ever said anything like that to me. It was outrageous. No matter how frightened he was that something would go wrong, a threat like that was utterly inexcusable. I just asked whether he still had all his marbles, laughed, and left it at that. What are you supposed to say to such a statement?

I can't think of any serious mistakes for which I alone was responsible. Once I didn't make a backup of the central server, and when it broke, Julian said, "WikiLeaks has only survived because I didn't trust you." Julian had a backup that we could use to reboot everything easily. No doubt, he hadn't made the copy out of fastidiousness but just because he distrusted people, including me. It was the server on which all our e-mails were stored. He wasn't a particularly careful person himself. Sometimes I thought when he talked to me, he was really talking about himself.

The absurd thing was that he was the one who was continually losing or forgetting things. And that was precisely what he was accusing me of. If Julian messed something up, on the other hand, something else was always the reason. He always had an elaborate explanation, sometimes one that cast him as the hero. When, in June 2009, he was due to be presented with Amnesty International's Media Award, he arrived in London three hours late. The leak for which the prize was awarded was about extrajudicial killings by the Kenyan police. Seventeen hundred people were murdered. Two human rights lawyers from a Kenyan legal-aid foundation had uncovered this and written a report on it. Not only did he miss the awards ceremony at which he was due to give a thank-you speech, but he also missed the interviews afterward that had been arranged. There were a lot of people in the audience we couldn't reach any other way. We expected this award to open a lot of doors for us, and it would take the wind out of the sails of some of our critics. Something Amnesty regarded as worthy of an award couldn't be that unethical. Two months before the award ceremony, Kamau Kingara, the director of the Kenyan foundation, and his program director, John Paul Oula, were gunned down in their car in Nairobi. The two of them were on their way to a Kenyan human rights commission, with which they had written their report.

We had only put the report on our website, making it accessible to a wider audience. We owed it to Kingara and Oula to accept the award on their behalf. It was the least we could do. Julian wrote a solemn press release in which he once again stressed their civic courage.

Julian's excuse for showing up late at the award ceremony was long-winded. It could have taken up several pages of a spy thriller. The only detail I can remember is that two police officers had allegedly followed him.

On another occasion, he explained that he had missed a connecting flight because he was busy solving an extremely difficult math problem. Although I spent a lot of time with him, I could never tell when he was trying to pull the wool over my eyes and when he was telling the truth.

I know at least three different versions of his past and the origins of his surname. There were stories of him having at least ten ancestors from various corners of the globe, from the South

Sea pirates to Irishmen. For a while, he even had business cards printed up with "Julian D'Assange" on them. He created a real sense of mystery about himself and constantly cloaked his past in new details. He was glad every time a journalist jotted them down. My first thought when I heard he was writing an autobiography was that they should put it in the fiction section!

Julian reinvented himself every day, like a hard drive that one kept on reformatting. Reset, reboot. Maybe he didn't know himself—who he was and where he came from. Maybe he had learned early on that he always had to cut himself free from women and friends, and this was easier if he could revise his personality and press the Reset button.

Julian was engaged in a constant battle for dominance—even with my cat, Mr. Schmitt. Mr. Schmitt is a lovable, lazy creature, a bit shy, with gray-and-white fur and an extremely laid-back way of walking. Unfortunately he also has a neurosis stemming from the time when Julian lived with me in Wiesbaden.

Julian was always attacking the poor animal. He would spread his fingers into a fork shape and pounce on the cat's neck. It was a game to see who was quicker. Either Julian would succeed in getting his fingers around the cat and pinning it to the floor, or the cat would drive Julian off with a swipe of its claws.

It must have been a nightmare for the poor thing. No sooner would Mr. Schmitt lie down to relax than the crazy Australian would be upon him. Julian preferred to attack at times when Mr. Schmitt was tired. "It's about training vigilance," Julian explained. Mr. Schmitt was a male cat, and male cats were supposed to be dominant. "A man must never forget he has to be the master of the situation," Julian proclaimed. I wasn't aware that anyone in my apartment or the courtyard had questioned Mr. Schmitt's masculinity. What's more, he was neutered.

Julian constantly attracted trouble. When we were on our way back from the International Journalism Conference in Perugia, Italy, in April 2009, there was an argument with a train conductor that almost cost us our flight back to Germany. We were under a lot of time pressure that day because we had to make a connecting flight in Rome. One train was delayed—an overhead transmission line had gone on the fritz—and we had to rearrange our plans and pay for a new ticket and a supplement on top of it. I took care of everything. I was the one who spent the agonizing minutes at the ticket counter while Julian sat on a bench waiting and watching our luggage. We ended up running across the platform and only managed to catch our new train at the very last minute because I had called out to the train staff from the escalators, "Don't leave; please wait!"

Our pulses racing, sweating profusely, we only just caught the train that the people in the station had told us was our final chance. It was in fact the very last train. We headed for two window seats, set down our backpacks on the free seats next to us, and stretched out our legs with a sigh.

A monster appeared: a badly shaved, slightly chubby Italian, who was working his way through the rows to our seats. The ticket inspector. Frowning, he examined our tickets and then thrust them back into our hands.

In bad English the Italian said that he was very sorry but we had obviously bought the wrong tickets. Nonetheless— abracadabra!—he said he could fix our problem for a small surcharge. I would have given in. But Julian completely lost it. He refused to pay the additional ten or fifteen euros and looked at the inspector with profound contempt.

The inspector definitely wasn't a particularly helpful person. He was simply a bad-tempered man in his midfifties who was doing his job and wanted to get back, as quickly as possible, to a card game with his colleagues, or whatever else awaited him in the ticket inspectors' compartment. We could have spent ages discussing why, through no fault of our own, we were being asked to pay up yet again and telling him what we thought more generally of his native land and its Mafia structures.

But we needed to get to Rome as quickly as possible in order to catch the cheap flight I had booked. Under the circumstances, I would have gladly paid the ridiculous surcharge and relaxed. However, Julian caused such a stir that the ticket inspector summoned the *carabinieri* at the next station. I was embarrassed—not least because there was someone sitting to our right who had also been at the conference in Perugia. Julian wasn't bothered about having an audience. It was almost as if he enjoyed putting on a small private theater performance.

We were now surrounded by the gruff inspector and two young police officers. "Your documents, please," demanded the female officer, who couldn't have been more than twenty years old but looked just as surly as the other two. I rummaged around in my pockets. Julian protested loudly, "We aren't going to show anyone here our documents."

I handed the woman my ID card. Julian crossed his arms and snorted contemptuously.

The three Italians looked at one another indecisively. They

would have liked to have thrown Julian off the train, but none of them wanted to make the first move. The young Australian was still sitting stretched out comfortably on his seat. They would have had to grab him by the arm and pull him out of his chair.

Julian was of the opinion that the inspector needed to be taught a lesson. That was one of his favorite sayings: "The man in the uniform has to learn his lesson."

He said that he wasn't tolerating anyone calling *his* authority into question and treating him without respect. Respect, respect, respect . . . he was always talking about respect. In this case, it was particularly pointless because the Italians probably didn't even understand the word. And Julian didn't respect anyone himself. It was getting on my nerves. I wanted to solve the problem. I didn't want to pay 700 euros for two new flights. I took advantage of the stalemate situation that had developed among the five of us. I gave the ticket inspector the money and steeled myself to put up with Julian's bad mood and preaching for the rest of the journey.

My will to make WikiLeaks an intrinsic part of my life was greater than my fear of being pushed around.

In 2009, when I appeared in a video interview for *Zeit Online* about the personal motives for my commitment to WikiLeaks, he accused me of being a media whore.

"Too much personality" was his reproach.

Julian told me we were too busy to have the time for lengthy interviews. After the *Zeit Online* video portrait, I tried to become less conspicuous. But this wasn't easy.

At the journalists' conference in Perugia, I had done a story with *Wired* magazine and a young freelance journalist, Annabel Symington.

Julian kept on throwing me dirty looks the whole time I was being interviewed. He said that he had heard me telling her that I was one of the "founders" of WikiLeaks. It was immensely important to him to keep stressing that he was the sole founder. I never said anything to the contrary. The competitiveness that lay behind all this was anathema to me. Even if I had experienced twinges of such feelings, I had suppressed them and been ashamed of myself.

Julian would later accuse me of playing power games. He was wrong. I didn't have a problem giving up power when it served our cause. On the contrary, I thought: Why should I burden myself with tons of responsibility when things functioned much better by sharing it? I'm a team player, not a loner like Julian. I can accept that other people do some things better than I do. In fact, there are a lot of them.

6

Financing WikiLeaks

SUCCESSFUL leaks that had attracted a lot of media coverage made themselves directly felt in our accounts. By 2008, we had three different PayPal accounts that people could use to make donations. For example, on March 1, 2008, as the leak appeared about Julius Bär, we had 1,900 euros in our main PayPal account. By March 3, that had already risen to 3,700, and by March 11, we had 5,000 euros.

Then, in June 2009, our only remaining active PayPal account was frozen. Money could still be paid into it, but we couldn't get any out.

We hadn't paid any attention to the account for months. It was only when PayPal informed us that we would no longer be able to withdraw money that we took a look at what had been paid in.

"You won't believe it," I wrote Julian in August 2009. "There are almost thirty-five thousand dollars in the account."

I was determined to unfreeze the account. Julian didn't think this was a priority and didn't see why we should bother with it.

PayPal wanted us to supply them with a certain document. We were registered as a nonprofit organization, but we had never officially applied for that status and were not qualified as a 501(c)(3) organization under US tax laws. Googling the term revealed that we weren't the first nonprofit organization to face this problem. PayPal regularly pestered its clients for this document. We registered as a business. That cost fees, but it saved a lot of time and energy. Even changing a comma in a PayPal contract is more trouble than it's worth. Life is too short.

I must have called the hotline thirty times and sent lots of e-mails back and forth. At a certain point I realized that PayPal wasn't a company with real flesh-and-blood employees. It was a machine. Admittedly, if you waited long enough on the hotline, you would end up speaking to real people at some point. But the Indian subcontractors, or whoever did these jobs for PayPal, could only tell you that you should please use the online system.

I think that PayPal's staff were just as much at the mercy of their own software as their clients. And this machinery neither knew pity nor recognized exceptional circumstances. The art of filling out the right fields remained a kind of arcane knowledge I would never be initiated into.

The system unfroze our assets briefly after we had turned the account into a business one and agreed to pay fees. For twenty-four hours, to be precise. Then the whole nonsense started again from the beginning. Once more a piece of information was missing. Once more it wasn't clear where this information had to be sent. Once more I got nowhere with the online system.

The dispute also created another problem. We weren't the only ones affected. All our accounts were maintained by volunteer supporters. For instance, a journalist had registered the frozen PayPal account for us. The contact person was a man in his late fifties from the Midwest in the United States—a down-to-earth guy who worked as a reporter for a local newspaper. At some point in the year, he had contacted us and asked if he could do anything to help. Because he hadn't suggested handling our finances, we gave him the job with the account. That was our logic at the time. Whoever wasn't interested in accounts was the best person to manage them. Whoever wasn't interested in personally influencing public opinion managed our chat room, and so on.

Our volunteer had no idea what to do, or where exactly the problem lay. It was all too much for him.

In September 2009, Julian got the "nanny" involved. The nanny was brought in whenever there was a job that Julian couldn't be bothered with or couldn't do himself. She sometimes arrived just before conferences to write his speeches. After other people and I left WikiLeaks, she was also the one who ended up traveling the world mediating between Julian and us and asking us not to damage the project by publicly criticizing it.

The nanny was an old friend of Julian's and was around forty—a pleasant but very resolute sort of person. For personal reasons I don't want to go into here, she would never want to talk about her contact with WL. That was likely a particular advantage she offered from Julian's perspective.

At any rate, the nanny had our American volunteer at his wit's end. What made the matter worse was that the time zones in which the two of them lived were so far apart that communication was only possible for one during the potential deep-sleep phase of the other. In addition, our poor volunteer was sick of describing the whole problem over again. In the end a journalist I knew from the *New York Times* came to the rescue. In the third week of September she went through official channels, getting in touch with PayPal directly and asking them why a project being supported by the *New York Times* had been frozen. Abracadabra! The account was released.

Things really turned nasty at that point. All of a sudden we had a bundle of money. But Julian and I had very different ideas about what to do with it.

I wanted to buy hardware—and not just because I really knew my way around that area. I wanted to get our infrastructure up to speed. This was desperately needed. As a result, breakdowns and security risks were inevitable. It made it far too easy for our adversaries. As long as everything was run on a single server, it would have been easy to break into WikiLeaks. That wouldn't have been so bad, but our documents were also on the server.

Julian had other plans, a lot more ostentatious plans. He talked about creating companies to better protect our donations from outside intervention. He said that it would set us back $15,000 in lawyers' fees just to register the companies in the United States.

Julian also had connections to some organizations that wanted to act as "fiscal sponsors." They were nonprofit organizations to which American donors could transfer money in order to avoid taxes. I don't know whose company Julian was keeping at the time, what kind of films he was watching, or more significantly, which documents on our site he had been reading a bit too closely, but suddenly all he could talk about was "front companies," "international law," and "offshore" firms. I imagined him sitting in front of me with his encrypted cell phone, his hands nonchalantly on his hips, his long white hair slicked back with gel, saying, "Hello, Tokyo, New York, Honolulu? Please transfer three million to the

Virgin Islands. Yes, thanks a lot. And don't forget to destroy the documents after the transaction has been completed. Burn them, please. And wipe up the ash and swallow it. OK? You know that I can't stand leftovers. . . ."

Whatever scenes Julian was playing out in his imagination, they fit his dream of an untouchable organization, an international network of firms, and the aura of someone invulnerable who juggled finances and firms all over the world and whom no one in the world could stop. Nonetheless, while it may not have been sexy, we could have used a few simple, practical things first of all.

My girlfriend at the time had bought us secure cell phones, or Cryptophones, as they're called. She shelled out an awful lot of money in one fell swoop. And I still feel bad now, when I think about how I slowly let our relationship die.

Months later, when we were in Iceland, I accidentally found out that Julian was trying to sell one of those astronomically expensive cell phones to one of our acquaintances—for 1,200 euros. Not only didn't the cell phones belong to him, but he wanted to sell one off at a hugely inflated price to someone who had no money for that kind of thing. Afterward, Julian gave away the cell phone to some seventeen-year-old guy he wanted to become more involved. Julian could be unself-consciously generous one minute, then really miserly a minute later.

In April 2008 we had opened an account with the UK-based money-transfer company Moneybookers. It was primarily intended to enable donors in the United States to transfer their money to us online. No one knew how much money was deposited in the Moneybookers account and what it was used for. Julian refused to allow me or other colleagues who joined later any access to the account.

Julian later opened another Moneybookers account in his own name. There was a direct link from our donation page to it. He refused to say what the account was for. It was closed in the fall of 2010, and later Julian publicly complained that WikiLeaks had had its money taken away. There is an e-mail Moneybookers sent to WikiLeaks on August 13, 2010, which was later quoted by the *Guardian* newspaper. According to it, the account was closed after examination by the security department at Moneybookers in order "to comply with money laundering and other investigations being carried out by government agencies." The account was indeed shut down. But every single cent had been withdrawn beforehand.

Ironically, Julian didn't really care about money per se. He never carried any on him, always letting other people pay. He justified this practice by saying that he didn't want anyone to trace his whereabouts from his ATM visits. Sometimes he would tell our helpers this—an hour after giving a press conference that had beamed his current location all around the world. They may well have swallowed it hook, line, and sinker. Women, in particular, liked to help Julian. They bought all sorts of things for him: clothes, rechargers, cell phones, coffee, flights, chocolate, new luggage, woolen socks.

Julian didn't give a hoot about status symbols. He may be different today, but back then, when we traveled together, he didn't own a watch, a car, or any designer clothing. He just didn't care.

Even his computer was ancient: a white iBook that was almost a museum piece. At the most, he would buy himself a new USB stick.

In addition to the donor accounts, we also considered other ways of raising money. One idea was to get paid for the leaked documents directly by auctioning off exclusive access to the material. A kind of eBay for WikiLeaks, you could say. In September 2008 we released a trial balloon. We announced on our website and in press releases that we were going to sell off to the highest bidder e-mails from Freddy Balzan, the speechwriter of Venezuelan president Hugo Chavez. The announcement got lots of media coverage in Latin America. That was not, however, because of the number of media organizations competing with one another to express interest in the documents. Instead, attention immediately shifted to our plan itself, and a critical debate ensued. We were accused of wanting to capitalize on the work of our sources. And there were complaints that only media organizations with money would be able to exploit this interesting material first. We just wanted to test the waters. In actual fact we didn't have the technical capacity to stage an auction of that kind at the time.

I tried to apply for money from the Knight Foundation. The John S. and James L. Knight Foundation, based in the United States, promotes exceptional journalistic projects. In 2009 alone, the foundation handed out more than $105 million. At the end of 2008 I submitted our first funding application, for $2 million. It got turned down in the third or fourth round of the multistage application procedure. When we received the news that we had made it into the second round, Julian announced that the $2 million grant was as good as in the bag. Well, not quite.

I tried again in 2009, submitting an application for half a million dollars. This application was very time-consuming, and Julian didn't help me. I spent two weeks working on the application with a volunteer. I had to answer eight questions about the motivation and inner structure of the project. One day before the deadline for submissions, Julian turned up with the nanny in tow.

The plan had been for the nanny to write the application on the eve of the deadline, but I had long since completed it. So we decided that we would make two applications. One was bound to be successful, or so the thinking went. Julian and the nanny tried to convince me that theirs would be the successful application. It was rejected in the first round. Mine got further, proceeding from round one to round two. Then, all of a sudden, we were in the penultimate round.

Later Julian would complain that I had tried to smuggle my name onto the application. That was a brazen reversal of the facts. Back in 2008, I had sat on the last day with the completed forms on my desk, wondering what to do about the signature. It was a real headache. We had to supply a real address, a real name, a permanent abode, and so on. . . . We didn't have an office that I could have used as an address. And Julian didn't have a fixed address anyway.

Time was running out, so I thought, Who cares about the United States? It really doesn't matter if I use my real name. I signed the application and sent it off. And in 2009 I did the same thing. I spent the next few days dreaming that WikiLeaks had been awarded the half million dollars and dreaming about all the things that we could afford with it. Just before going to sleep I thought about how we could set up the most sophisticated security equipment—only the best: half a rack in a properly air-conditioned data center, with an electric generator and a network as well as a terminal server for accessing other servers if there was a problem. And the servers would be from the most recent generation, not from two generations past.

I carried on dreaming. Of renting an office and entrusting people with specific tasks. Of paying ourselves salaries. I would have preferred never to return to the company I worked for, with its Excel sheets, Tuesday meetings, and my secret telephone conferences in the storeroom on the eighth floor.

The application procedure went on for weeks. The Knight Foundation asked for additional paperwork and wanted to invite us to the last round at MIT in Boston. They wanted to meet us personally and put questions to our "board."

The advisory board was a daring construction that had been set up before my time. Only one of the eight people listed as belonging to our advisory board publicly acknowledged a link to us—that was C J Hinke, a Net activist from Thailand. Journalists dug up every single one of the ostensible board members over time. The Chinese ones immediately denied any connection. Julian dismissed this with the words "Of course, they can't publicly acknowledge their link to us." Ben Laurie denied on several occasions ever having played an advisory role. Phillip Adams at least said that he had agreed on some occasion but had not been able to contribute to the project for health reasons.

The foundation would no doubt have found it useful to have met with the inner circle of WikiLeaks on at least one occasion, but it was impossible to find a time that suited us all. The e-mails went back and forth for ages. The foundation must have thought that we were either completely arrogant or extremely disorganized. Both were true. That's why I put myself at their disposal. I wanted to give our contacts the feeling that we had things under control. Julian wrote me an angry e-mail afterward: "You're not the applicant."

Later he told the others that I had tried to force my way onto the application. My God! We could have put our energy to better use by combining forces to put together a great presentation. The application failed to clear the final hurdle.

Quitting My Day Job

7

TO me, it was quite clear that our aim was to earn a living from WikiLeaks one day. It would mean that no one would need to turn tricks on the side. That was a constant problem. We needed a lot more people. And we needed a lot more time. But we lacked both because almost all of us had to earn money outside WikiLeaks.

In my eyes, not being able to do the work that you knew was more meaningful was a kind of prostitution. Of course, I know I'm not the only one in the world unable to do what he loves most.

There was only one person who received money for his services directly from WikiLeaks, a technician who is still with the project. Perhaps he's stayed on out of a sense of obligation because of that money. And once we paid a journalist about 600 euros for writing us an extensive analysis about the bank leaks. We thought at the time that we should have engaged someone specifically to carry out much more probing research. Back in 2008, 600 euros was a lot of money for us.

Increasingly, my job was getting on my nerves. Investing my energies on behalf of my clients was leading me nowhere. What

was the point of Opel producing more cars, or another of my customers boosting his turnover? That didn't make the world a better place. I felt that people with certain qualifications also had a
responsibility to invest them for the good of society. Every minute
I spent in the office seemed like a waste of time. I concentrated on
doing my work as efficiently as possible. That wasn't a problem in
a big company in which project phases were generously calculated,
particularly when you work more quickly than most of the others.

I worked for WikiLeaks at night and for the company during
the day, increasingly from home. Sometimes the telephone would
wake me at eleven a.m. with an important customer on the line.
I had invariably forgotten that I had an appointment for a telephone conference. Wearing just my underwear and old socks, and
having just been torn from a deep sleep, I would stumble over a
package of secret military documents spread out over the floor
and plop down onto my beanbag chair. And then I would explain
to top managers of leading international companies what a brilliant job we could do optimizing their data centers. Afterward I
would return to the documents, the secret-service papers and the
corruption cases due to be published next on the website. The
quality of my work remained impeccable. My parents had raised
me to be conscientious, and that's something that sticks with you.

In mid-2008 I was in Moscow for my employer for four weeks.
My job was meant to be installing a data center in an office building. When I got there, it became apparent that the whole business
was going horribly wrong.

I stayed on the northeastern outskirts of the city in a Holi-
day Inn by Sokolniki Park, and it took forty-five minutes on the
subway every day to get to where I was working. Because I was

the only non-Russian—that is, the only one there who could be trusted—I quickly got charged with doing all sorts of things. The customer called me every day. I was working round the clock, and was forever trying to protect hardware worth almost a million dollars from dust. Either a workman would be sandpapering the walls in front of the server room, or an air-conditioning unit in the ceiling would be leaking.

The building site was a nightmare. The poorly paid workmen simply hid the rubble and the garbage in the cavity between the floor and the ceiling of the unit below, and the heating pipes had sprung their first leaks even before they were finished, because people had been walking around too much on top of them. I had developed blood blisters on my feet. I managed to wear out a pair of Doc Martens in Moscow. The city was a real pain in the ass.

Once, I took a short break to experience another side of the city. I went to see my former exchange partner, with whom I had lived when I visited Russia in the twelfth grade. Vladimir* had studied law. When I asked him what exactly his current job involved, he said "doing people favors." He had four girlfriends and had bought each of them a car and an apartment. What impressed me most was the letter he had in his car from the police chief saying, for all intents and purposes, "Please leave this man alone."

I'm not usually a nervous passenger. But I clung to the handle above the window as Vladimir jerked his car into the right-turn lane at a hundred kilometers per hour, or when he created a lane of his own, firmly convinced that everyone else would make way for him and knowing that he would win the traffic case if it ever came to court.

From my office window, I could see several huge building

sites. Moldavian workers were constructing some record-breaking buildings. Meanwhile, to my left was the highest building in Europe; to my right, the second-highest tower in the world, if I remember correctly. The laborers lived in small container cities—the Russian version of townships—that were fenced off with barbed wire. More than fifty laborers died in accidents on one building site since the beginning of the construction works. It's a disgrace that we didn't publish a single document about the conditions in Russia in all those years. One of the reasons was that we received so little material, and then there was the language barrier. Neither Julian nor I nor anyone from the inner circle could understand Russian. You can say what you like about many people's number-one enemy, the United States, but in Moscow the situation was also acute. I would have loved to have had more time for WikiLeaks during those weeks. I did at least manage to meet with Transparency International in Moscow and to give an interview at the German public television station ARD's Moscow studio.

The first wave of firings at my employer started taking place at that time. Our labor-advisory committee sent around an e-mail, offering staff the chance to get some advice. A short time later, we received an e-mail from management, warning us not to count the quarter of an hour we spent with the committee as part of our official working day. We were constantly being bombarded with petty-minded nonsense and preachy bullshit—for example, reminders that Christmas Eve was also half a working day, or that pens and erasers were company property.

I was furious. I was working sixteen to eighteen hours a day, and the company was insinuating that we were trying to cheat them out of fifteen minutes of paid work. So I wrote an e-mail and sent it to all the company's German staff. As sender, I entered the address of the management, and I cc'd all our bosses. In the e-mail I asked the managing director not to assume that others shared his own work ethic. I added that it would also be nice if the advisory committee could show a bit of backbone. I sent the e-mail via a network printer. I knew its IP address because it was the printer in the hall outside my office in Rüsselsheim.

It didn't take long before a chat box opened on my computer. A colleague who was part of management's inner circle had sent me an agitated inquiry. She told me that they had a problem and asked whether I could briefly help, as I knew a lot about security and that kind of thing. I pretended to be amazed.

"Unbelievable!" I wrote.

I investigated the case thoroughly and reminded her that I had already pointed out the security problems linked to network printers on a number of occasions.

"Isn't it possible to find out who sent the e-mail?" she wanted to know.

"Unfortunately not," I wrote. "I also have an awful lot to do here. Sorry."

I signed off cordially and returned my attention to the Russian building site again.

Some of my colleagues back home soon developed a blind hatred toward whoever had sent that e-mail. They were worried that they might be fingered for it and were sure they would get fired any day. In particular, people who were always complaining about management were suddenly shitting their pants.

It was very amusing to see just how amateurishly the subsequent police investigation about my e-mail proceeded. In their attempt to track down the culprit, the police sealed everything off and dusted for fingerprints on all the printers and photocopiers. They removed the hard drives from all the nearby computers and took them in for forensic examination. Of course, nothing ever came of it.

In early 2009 I decided to resign once and for all. Normally, I wouldn't have been a candidate for layoffs, but because I had come forward of my own free will and I was young and single, the company could hardly say no. I managed to negotiate a year's pay as a severance package. On January 31, 2009, I left for good. Finally I could devote my entire energy round the clock to WikiLeaks. The first thing I did with my severance money was to buy us six new laptops and a few new telephones. At first, my parents just couldn't understand why I had given notice. To them it sounded very risky to be relinquishing a safe job, a pension, and all that. Nonetheless, fundamentally, they've always supported whatever I have done. My mother, in particular, had long since realized that I wanted to do something that I believed would benefit society, and it was clear to her that any attempts to stop me would only be counterproductive.

At that time, I thought that we would be able to develop the project to a point where we could pay ourselves a modest salary. So quitting my job didn't seem all that adventurous. Everything felt right.

8

The Censorship Debate

IN 2008, we began publishing Internet filter lists. They're used to block websites, for instance, when parents want to protect their children from certain types of content. The first lists were from Thailand. In this case, it was clear that they were being deployed for political purposes. The regime was using the main filter to undermine criticism of the royal family. Websites with antigovernment content were being suppressed along with pornographic material.

Soon we began receiving leaked filter lists from democratic countries as well, including Norway, Finland, Denmark, Italy, and Australia. These lists were primarily intended to restrict the flow of child pornography, and parents were able to install the filters on their own computers and those used by their children. This is, no doubt, a noble endeavor. It only became a measure of censorship when lawmakers tried to make the filters mandatory for *all* Internet users. Proponents argue that filters are the only effective means of combating child pornography, but that's a fallacy that has been thoroughly disproven.

Our leaks revealed that even the best filter list was wrong about two-thirds of the sites it identified as dangerous. Some of the lists were mistaken up to 90 percent of the time. With the Finnish list, only a very small percentage of the sites identified had anything to do with child pornography. The facts about the lists played a major role in the anticensorship protest movement.

Not only were the systems poor; they could be easily misused for political purposes—and not just in dictatorships and monolithic states like China or North Korea. In Finland, Matti Nikki—one of the country's best-known bloggers and a critic of Internet censorship—fell victim to the lists of prohibited content. After he had published the list of banned sites in Finland, he suddenly found his own IP address on it.

The Australian lists contained a dentist's business page and some antiabortion sites, as well as home pages created by homosexuals and religious minorities. Our leak coincided with elections in Australia. The Australian government was trying to make Internet filters mandatory, and initially the politicians tried to deny the list we had leaked was the same one upon which their proposed legislation was based. Ironically, we soon received another list that was very similar to the first one—but with corrections on those points that had come in for heavy public criticism.

In late April 2009, Ursula von der Leyen, who was then Germany's minister of Family Affairs, presented a first draft for what she called the Access Impediment Law. Even the scientific service of the German parliament criticized it as being probably unconstitutional. Nonetheless, I think the draft legislation would have been waved through if we hadn't succeeded in focusing public attention on the topic.

But as was so often the case, the name WikiLeaks wasn't at the center of the public debate. For this to become a political issue, someone else needed to take up the cause as her own. In this case, and luckily for us, that person was a young woman from Berlin.

Franziska Heine is an anticensorship activist who had stumbled over the censorship issue in a blog and immediately drafted an online petition that was to become the most successful of its kind ever in Germany. Within the space of days, Franziska had become a public figure, at least in those political and journalistic circles concerned with questions of censorship. Major German newspapers and TV shows wanted to interview her. Whenever we went out somewhere together, her cell phone wouldn't stop ringing, and she talked to the press every lunch hour.

I'd met Franziska via e-mail. After she drafted her petition, I wrote to her and asked her if we could cooperate. Her response was enthusiastic, concluding with the words "We should meet up." A few days later, I was sitting on a train to Berlin.

Franziska is a very open person. The first time we met, we took a three-hour-long walk along the Spree River, talking all the while. Most of the time, she had a very friendly, somewhat mischievous look on her face. What's more, she had a talent for asking the right questions. It was fun conversing with her. I only wished I hadn't brought along my messenger bag. For security reasons, I never left my two laptops and my cell phone unattended at home. They lay heavy in my bag and made every step a physical trial for my right shoulder.

Later I went with her to a popular outdoor techno bar called the Club of the Visionaries. We sat on its wooden dock, rocked back and forth to the beats, and stared at the Spree. Other bloggers and Net activists joined us, and of course, a lively discussion ensued. Franziska was very committed, at least as much as I was, to our mutual cause.

I don't know whether she enjoyed being the center of attention. Along with her anticensorship work, she had a normal full-time job as a project manager with a telecommunications firm. She was the perfect spokeswoman—someone who hadn't yet made a name for herself in the realm of Internet issues. She couldn't be accused of having a political agenda or being tempted to misuse our cause to further her own career. Because she didn't grasp all the details of many technical questions, she would seek my advice when she was invited to talk to the press. I was glad to help her, not only because I enjoyed providing the buzzwords and serving as a walking, talking technical dictionary, but because it gave me access to political decision makers.

Together, we put up posters for the large antigovernment surveillance demonstration "Freedom, Not Fear" in Berlin in 2009, and she also attended the major hackers' conference in the Netherlands, HAR (Hacking At Random). Nowadays, I don't have that much contact with her. I think she's probably glad to have more time to devote to her career and her private life. Back in 2009, quite a lot of people were interested in censorship questions, but it was hard to get them to work with us. I believe they thought that because they'd been involved longer, they owned the topic. A lot of the discussions revolved not around the issues, but around whose name would be at the bottom of what press release.

Once Franziska was invited to debate the issue with Ursula von der Leyen. The event was moderated by Kai Biermann and Heinrich Wefing—an online journalist and a print editor, respectively, for the highbrow weekly newspaper *Die Zeit*. Franziska asked me to come along. The journalists agreed to this, but they insisted that my answers be ascribed to her.

My impression was that the journalists thought I was a bit of a nuisance. While they did ask me if I wanted a coffee or some water, and I was given a chair, both men were clearly focused on Franziska. Whenever she said anything, they would nod and smile in her direction.

They wanted to know how she had come to start her petition. Every time I would interject with something technology-specific, they would say, "Too much detail; too technical." I asked myself how people were supposed to understand the overarching issues if they weren't prepared to get a grip on the technical details. But the journalists were primarily interested in getting the personal story behind the issue.

Normally, I have no interest in confirming quotes. I even mentioned to Wefing that I thought this practice was a blight upon German journalists—a sentiment for which other journalists, I think, would have stood up and given me a spontaneous hug. But Wefing said he thought that it was a specifically German virtue, and that no one would talk to journalists anymore if the practice were not followed.

In retrospect, we made a mistake when we gave *Die Zeit* the OK to print the first transcript of the discussion as it was sent to us. While we were agreeing that it was a balanced representation of the debate, the transcript was also being sent to the other side, and von der Leyen's press spokesman demanded a number of ex post facto changes. What was ultimately printed was a distortion of the debate, to our disadvantage. That was very irritating.

Later, we had a second appointment with the minister. Ursula von der Leyen's office is located in a massive, gray concrete building not far from Alexanderplatz. Franziska and I took the elevator up, and someone collected us and took us to a conference room. The space was about half the size of a school classroom; in the middle there was a cluster of tables and chairs. The minister was waiting there, along with some others: Annette Niederfranke, ministerial director and director of Division 6: Child and Youth Aid; one of her assistants; and Jens Flossdorf, von der Leyen's press spokesman. We already knew him from the *Zeit* interview. But there was also someone else in attendance, with whom we definitely hadn't reckoned. An eight-year-old girl named Lisa*.

We took our seats at one end of the ensemble of tables, directly across from the little brown-haired girl, who was concentrating on drawing things with wax crayons on white sheets of paper. Lisa, we were told, was the daughter of Annette Niederfranke's assistant. The father was on a business trip and so after school, there was no choice but to bring Lisa to her mother at the office. No one else at the ministry was available to mind her, so she would have to sit there at the table while we discussed child pornography.

"That won't be a problem, will it?" Ursula von der Leyen said in an overly friendly tone, assuring us, as though we had said anything to the contrary, that Lisa was a well-behaved child. "She's only drawing some funny, colorful pictures."

Since there was no choice but for her to be sitting there, we were not supposed to use the "C-word," by which she meant "child pornography." We didn't have to use this "terrible word," von der Leyen said, repeating, "this terrible, terrible, word." She shot us a look of dismay and added, "We all know what this is about."

Then she nodded gravely. The discussion could begin.

It lasted at least two hours. The whole time, Ursula von der Leyen talked about the "C-word"—unlike the woman to her right, the young assistant to the director of Division 6. She simply spat out the phrase "child pornography." But she was only Lisa's mother. The whole thing was like a cabaret sketch.

Then it was time for Lisa to go to bed. The appointment was over. "Thank you," the minister said. "It was a pleasure. Can you see yourselves out?"

For the duration of the meeting, von der Leyen's tone was very calm and measured, and every word and gesture seemed aimed at demonstrating how cheerful and nice she found herself. For our part, we were concerned not to scare little Lisa. There was no chance for either of us to pound our fist on the table and say, "Sorry, but all the bullshit you guys are planning won't do a thing to stop a single pedophile!"

Whether or not this was some clever PR strategy, afterward we felt we had been morally blackmailed and kicked ourselves for not having simply broken off the discussion.

But at least we understood a bit better how Ursula von der Leyen ticked. She had told us how awful it was for her when people asked her at international conferences why Germany wasn't taking sufficient steps against child pornography. That was her main concern. It seemed to me that she only wanted to do something to prove that she was doing something. What, exactly, she did seemed to be of secondary importance.

Our opposition to this nonsensical piece of legislation was nonetheless one of the most politically effective actions of my time with WL. It was a perfect example of the speed with which political pressure can be brought to bear. We had the facts and, in Franziska, a charismatic activist. Four weeks later we were sitting at a table with Germany's minister of Family Affairs.

Of the two sorts of political activism, this was the one I preferred. You could criticize after the fact, as we had done with Toll Collect and the German pharmaceutical company, that something had gone wrong. Or you could make your influence felt in an ongoing process, as was the case here. We also learned from this experience that you have to overcome a certain hurdle of media attention in order to get things moving.

At HAR in Vierhouten in 2009, we tried to transfer the political momentum we felt we had built up in Germany to a larger forum. Our goal was to found a global political movement against Internet censorship.

The Hacking At Random conference is like a Woodstock for hackers—a giant campsite festival that takes place every four years at different locations in the Netherlands. HAR is a good place to make new contacts and launch new topics. In addition, there are lots of panel discussions and debates. Julian and I were scheduled to hold three lectures, and one of them was on censorship.

My girlfriend, one of our technicians, and I arrived in Vierhouten in a large white Mercedes van a week before the official start of camp on August 13. We had a lot of stuff with us, but I was most proud of the light-blue flag with the WL logo I had ordered over the Internet. It was two meters long and was hoisted atop a six-meter flagpole. We also had two party tents, my mobile

solar battery unit, a bunch of lights, and a mirrored disco ball—
along with a refrigerator, a hammock, an inflatable armchair, and
a mattress.

The conference grounds were located in a woodsy area normally used as a campsite for vacationing families. We all pitched
in to get things ready, distributing extension cords for power, setting up the data network, putting up the lecture tents, and roll-
ing out miles of conventional and fiber-optic cables and threading
them through the trees so that people wouldn't trip over them. In
ten days, we built a complete tent city with everything we needed,
including a ten-gigabyte Internet connection that would divert
most of the entire digital traffic of Europe to Vierhouten. Setting
up camps like this was more fun for me than practically anything
else. It was great to get some fresh air and exercise and to deal
with real people and objects.

The weather was generally splendid, but one night there was
a brief cloudburst. The rain got into the batteries attached to the
solar unit, causing a short circuit, and our facilities almost burned
to the ground. We only noticed it the following morning.

Julian arrived two days before his first lecture. He set up his
tent in a remote corner of the grounds and then proceeded to
meander about. Lending a hand with preparations wasn't his
thing.

At HAR, everyone runs around with DECT telephones connected to their own network. You can call anyone anywhere in
the world, but you can also use them to make contact with all the
other conference participants and call up friends you've lost in the
masses of people.

I was reminded of a lecture we had held in Berlin in 2008.

Someone from the audience had recognized Julian onstage and called out, "Hey, Mendax!" You could see from Julian's face how glad he was that someone had remembered his former hacker pseudonym. At the Berlin congress in December 2007, too, he had probably been the biggest hacker by far, and he paraded around in keeping with his status. I think he was a bit disappointed that year that no one at that event had recognized him.

You could reserve a four-digit code for the DECT telephones, and for Julian I had selected 6639: MNDX. I think that made him really happy. My code was 5325: LEAK. Unfortunately, his phone never rang. But he also never charged its battery, and he didn't seem to pay it any attention.

Amidst all the official events at HAR, there was always a party going on somewhere. We had the disco ball and music in our tent, and every evening we'd cook together. There were never fewer than twenty people, if only because we were so well equipped. My girlfriend found HAR relaxing. She was glad we could be together for a few days and lounged around in the hammock, painting her toenails in rainbow colors.

She was also a big help. She collected money for shopping and helped with the cooking. Everyone liked her. But someone who was even happier about our field trip was our technician. He enjoyed being out in the fresh air, and he struck up new friendships and was taking things easy. I remember thinking that we should all get together and do things more often instead of sitting in front of our computers all the time. And how nice it was to look at trees.

Marvin Minsky, the artificial intelligence expert who was one of the first to advance the thesis that our brains would someday be directly connected to our computers, was once asked when we would be living in an entirely virtual world. He answered to the effect that this would never happen as long as we looked up after two hours in front of a computer, saw a tree, and admired what a wonderfully detailed thing it is.

Julian then decided he wanted to hold a new lecture, and he didn't want to agree on everything in advance with me, even though we staged our presentations in tandem. He went to a hotel to better prepare, going through every minute detail with a female acquaintance. It was difficult to reach him there.

On the one hand, I was glad he'd shown up two days in advance, and not two minutes, as was his wont. On the other, I wouldn't have minded consulting with him. The constant spontaneously kamikaze performances onstage were beginning to fray my nerves, although they did force me to develop a talent for improvisation. Today, I often go into speaking dates unprepared. I can talk about some topics in my sleep. Afterward, people tell me I was easy to listen to because everything sounded so fresh.

I have Julian to thank for that. Ever since we started holding joint lectures, I've lost my fear that something will go wrong, that the projector will catch fire or the stage will collapse. Everything that can happen already has. Sometimes, if there was no room on the official program for us but we thought we needed to be part of an event, we would just hijack a stage. That was what we did, for instance, at the Global Voices Summit in Budapest in 2008. Global Voices is an international network of bloggers who translate, defend, and report on blog journalism and blogs. The conference was an exciting platform for us, since members of Global Voices could have helped further spread our leaks. So we simply created our own slot on the program, distributing flyers in advance and then grabbing the podium immediately after an official lecture was over.

Following the conference, we were approached by someone from George Soros's Open Society Institute. He had found our lecture interesting, and we talked about possibly financing our project through the OSI. Julian once told me that the OSI had asked us for a wish list and that we shouldn't be too modest in drawing it up. As far as I know, nothing ever came of this.

Our lecture on Internet censorship, one of three we held at HAR, was our opportunity to call forth a new international movement. There was a podium discussion moderated by me, and with me onstage were Julian; Rop Gonggrijp, a Dutch Net activist who would later help us with the "Collateral Murder" video; Franziska; a representative from the German data-protection association Foebud; and a whistle-blower formerly of MI6 in Great Britain. We all agreed in theory. Everywhere in the world politicians were coming up with censorship laws, and everywhere in the world people were protesting against them. It would be sensible to act globally and coordinate resistance centrally.

After our lecture, many of the audience members came up to us and said they'd like to get involved. We created a mailing list for the global anticensorship movement. But that was as far as it went.

I think what the movement lacked was a leader of the pack, an outstanding individual who could make the cause his own and get people to follow him. Initiatives like this always needed someone crazy enough to be the vanguard. Who could have known that better than me?

Along with trying to found a global anticensorship movement, I had assigned myself another job, perhaps the toughest of my life. I had gotten T-shirts printed with the WL logo. Because I thought our logo stood out best that way and because I wanted to save two cents per T-shirt, I'd ordered them in white. That was idiotic. Who buys white T-shirts? Especially in a social clique where black T-shirts are something of a dress code. I myself had never worn a white T-shirt in my entire life!

Now I was sitting on 250 shirts, the equivalent of almost four moving boxes' full. Unpacked and piled up, they measured a frightening three meters. And I had to get rid of the pile. Nowadays, WL fans would no doubt rush to buy them for ten times what I was asking, but back then no one was interested. I literally had to stop people in their tracks as they were passing our stand and beg them to trade 5 euros from their wallets for a T-shirt. Unfortunately, my companions weren't any better at this than I was. If we'd been forced to go into retail, we would have starved. My girlfriend was far too honest to convince someone that he absolutely had to have such an ugly article of clothing, and Julian preferred to engage potential customers in deep conversations about the state of the world. He stood there talking and talking, occasionally getting into an argument, until no one was thinking about T-shirts anymore.

I narrowly avoided losing money on the shirts. One thing was clear: WL merchandising was not going to save us from our financial problems.

• • •

A year later we received a prize—an artistic award from Ars
Electronica, a media festival that takes place every year in Linz,
Austria. As far as I was concerned, this was ridiculous. And the
story also began on a comic note.

To win a prize at Ars Electronica, you actually have to apply,
and every year thousands of artists do precisely that. With us,
things worked the other way around. We received an e-mail from
the organizers. At first, they just sent us some information about
the prize. We deleted it. Art didn't interest us in the slightest.
What did these people want from us?

As more and more e-mails appeared, we began to think, Maybe
these people want to give us a prize. After all, the requests for us
to apply had come far in advance of any jury meetings or selection decisions. We didn't put much past the intellectual, high-tech
art scene. We read through the description of the prizewinning
works from the previous year. That confused us even more. The
descriptions sounded like willfully nonsensical cabaret numbers
or pieces of satire, but they were apparently written in complete
seriousness. Little of it was socially relevant in the slightest. How
did WL fit in here?

But because the curators of Ars Electronica had been so persistent I submitted a few pages of general information about WL.
And—surprise, surprise!—we received an invitation to the awards
ceremony in Linz on September 4, 2009.

Only one hotel room was provided, so Julian and I had to
sleep in a double bed. But compared to the holes we usually slept
in when we had public dates, the Hotel Wolfinger was like the

Ritz. It had a rustic Austrian charm but was also totally stylish. I felt like I should be taking off my shoes whenever I trod on the parquet floor in our room—and tidying up before I left it. Whenever Julian and I spent five minutes anywhere, it looked as though a suitcase full of clothes had exploded, with some cables and telephones thrown in for decoration. But I consoled myself with the thought that the other artists invited to Linz probably weren't any neater than we were.

Upon our arrival, we had hoped to meet a couple of rich art mavens with whom we could network and who would give us money. We were living hand to mouth back then. I had to tape the battery of my laptop to its case because its holder was broken. And a fresh pair of shoes would have made a new man out of Julian.

But we did our best to get dressed up for the art scene. I had a pair of black leather shoes on that were in pretty good shape. Julian wore a tailored cotton overcoat. It was a bit too small and was probably meant for a woman, but it did lend him a sophisticated touch. He looked a bit like Phantomias, Donald Duck's superhero alter ego in the German comic books, getting ready to fly, but he also made a worldly impression.

A short time before the awards ceremony, which was held in Linz's Bucknerhaus, we got separated. Perhaps Julian had decided to take a walk along the river or had gone back to the hotel, because he didn't like the scene at Bucknerhaus.

He didn't miss much. To my eyes, the projects that were given awards were completely senseless, and the moderator who eventually announced that we had taken second place didn't even mention us by name. The giant ballroom where the ceremony was held was full of gentlemen in suits and ladies in evening gowns, and the first row was occupied by sponsors, taking up at least twenty seats, with the artists in their required idiosyncratic attire between them. The whole thing was a waste of time for us because no one learned who we were. So much for the art mavens who were supposed to stuff our pockets with large-denomination bills.

The accompanying exhibit also struck me as being completely over the top. I did buy a watch that ran on bio-energy from a plant, but that was the only project I liked. Otherwise, people just ran around, pompously talking about their banal works and praising themselves to the skies. In the cellar there was a presentation with a couple of photos and some stand-up posters from us. I had tinkered with the surrounding Internet terminals so that the browsers only called up the WikiLeaks page. But even that didn't attract anyone's attention.

I caught a plane the following day, earlier than planned, because the entire event got on my nerves so much. Julian stayed until Monday. The prizewinners were supposed to be given a chance to present their projects and talk to one another. Around noon there was a press conference, in the same auditorium as the night before, but with a far smaller audience. Every prize recipient was allotted five minutes to speak. The organizers made the mistake of giving Julian the microphone first.

"Are there any representatives from the media in the room?" Julian asked.

A few people, roughly half of the audience, raised their hands.

"What luck," Julian said. "I was afraid I was going to get stuck with a bunch of art wankers again."

Around half of the audience, the same half that had raised their hands, laughed. Julian then got going, explaining to the giggling journalists and the insulted artists how WikiLeaks—and the entire world—functioned. It was forty-five minutes before he wound up.

9

Heroes in Iceland

I N the summer of 2009, with the global financial crisis still
in full swing, someone sent us material from the Kaupthing
Bank, at the time the largest bank in Iceland. The document, which we published on August 1 of that year, showed that
the bank's partners and close associates had been given credit on
extremely favorable terms just before the bank had filed for insol-
vency. The media would subsequently speak of the bank being
"plundered" by its owners. The recipients of the loans hadn't put
down much in the way of security, if anything at all, but had
received sums in the high millions.

The revelations made people in Iceland take to the streets, and
there was outrage in England and the Netherlands, too, where
many of the debtors were located. Icelanders realized that they
had been systematically exploited. Their state and their social
security system had gone bankrupt while financial third parties
had gleefully filled their pockets.

A short time later, a group of Icelanders got in touch with us.
One of them was a student named Herbert Snorrason. Together
with a group at his university called FSFI, he was planning a

conference on digital liberties and asked whether we'd like to attend. I immediately said yes.

Julian initially hesitated. He always agreed to attend events only at the last minute, after I'd planned and organized every-thing. Maybe he was convinced when I mentioned that Iceland, statistically, has the highest proportion of attractive women in the world. I had read that somewhere.

I was glad to go with him to the conference in Iceland. We always had a lot of fun whenever we were together. What was beginning to irritate me, though, was his way of playing the boss. He always shook hands with people first, for instance, saying, "I'm Julian Assange, and this is my colleague." I would have never done that. It would have never occurred to me to say of Julian: "This is my colleague."

We flew to Iceland in November 2009. I took a plane from Berlin; Julian arrived from somewhere else. I had booked us into the Baldursbra, a cozy, completely untrendy guesthouse in down-town Reykjavík that was run by a Frenchwoman. Julian and I shared a corner room on the third floor.

After my arrival, I immediately went out into the streets and found a restaurant. Herbert joined me, together with a friend of his named Smári. I don't recall the name of the restaurant, but the fish soup was excellent. I also learned you can get a malt beer, and a tasty one at that, wherever you go in Iceland.

I knew Herbert through the chat room. He appeared there shortly after the Kaupthing leak and had soon taken over the task of answering questions from newcomers. Herbert is a thoughtful, pleasant guy with a fine sense of humor. He's in his midtwenties, wears a funny-looking, often overgrown beard, and studies history and Russian at the University of Iceland. One of his favorite quotes is "Property is theft" from the nineteenth-century French economist and anarchist Pierre-Joseph Proudhon. To characterize himself, he also quotes the German anarcho-syndicalist Rudolf Rocker: "I am an Anarchist not because I believe Anarchism is the final goal, but because there is no such thing as a final goal."

Herbert knew the anarchist classics that are also on my unofficial list of favorite works of world literature, and I was excited to find a kindred spirit in such a faraway place. I think Proudhon's *What Is Property?* is the most important book ever written, and I'd brought a new edition of the author's works, containing previously unpublished letters, with me to Iceland. They had been on my nightstand since Christmas, along with Jeremy Scahill's *Blackwater,* P. W. Singer's *Corporate Warriors,* and Gustav Landauer's *The Revolution,* and I was hoping to find a bit of time to make a dent in them. I could philosophize for hours with Herbert. As a historian, he knew a lot of things that I, as a computer scientist, didn't have a clue about, and he was mightily impressed when I showed him my new Proudhon edition.

Smári was new to me. He studied information technology and was co-organizing the conference with Herbert. He had disheveled blond hair and was very sociable and educated, but unfortunately also a little scatterbrained and unreliable at times. He was half Irish and had the coolest name imaginable: Smári McCarthy. Smári means "shamrock" in Icelandic. His parents had played a bit of a joke on him. He took it with humor as he did everything in life.

We talked until the owner of the restaurant came up to our table and said he wanted to close. Julian arrived on the last plane in and joined us in the guesthouse. It was on this evening that the idea of making Iceland into a free-press haven was born.

Officially we were there for the conference only, but news of our arrival had gotten around. Iceland is a small country. We had become something like folk heroes for leaking the machinations at the Kaupthing Bank. The Icelandic TV station RUV had wanted to report on the leak on August 1, but five minutes before airtime, a legal injunction arrived, prohibiting the report from being broadcast. The editors at the station refused to be silenced and broadcast our Web address in large letters instead. Afterward, practically every Icelander knew WikiLeaks, and a lot of them looked at the original documents on our page.

The following day, we received an invitation from Iceland's most famous talk-show host, Egill Helgason. He wanted us to be guests on his afternoon show on November 28. We told him about our idea of making Iceland into a safe haven for freedom of the press, with the most progressive media laws in the world, and asked him if we could announce it on his show.

In truth, neither is the idea new nor did it come from us. It originated in science-fiction literature, in Neal Stephenson's 1999 novel *Cryptonomicon,* among other places. The establishment of a data haven plays a central role in the story, which revolves around an attempt to make the fictional Asian island of Kinakuta into a place where avenues of communication are beyond the control of any authority in the world. The novel features, among other things, a deciphered encryption system used by the German army, Nazi gold, and clandestine military operations. Along with the works of Solzhenitsyn, *Cryptonomicon* is one of Julian's favorite books, and he has adopted a number of words from it. For example, the word "honing"—a technical term in engineering. It describes a process whereby one continually works on and fine-tunes a seemingly objective conclusion. If he wanted to improve a phrase, he would talk about it needing to be honed, like a piece of metal.

He also swapped his hacker nickname Mendax for "Proff," possibly in homage to the character Prof from the novel. That character is based on a real-life figure, the British mathematician Alan Turing. In computer circles, he's considered one of the leading minds of the twentieth century because he wrote the software for one of the first computers, and was instrumental in cracking the Nazis Enigma Code.

In our idea of a free-media haven, Iceland would serve as an "offshore" island—akin to those offshore locales that offer particularly favorable conditions to businesses—with laws favoring media companies and information-service providers. In many countries, there is no freedom of the media. Even in democratic nations, journalists are warned, punished, and even forced to name their sources. In our concept, media and providers would be able to move their headquarters, if only virtually, to Iceland and enjoy the protection of especially progressive laws.

Iceland was already dramatically expanding its computer centers and was extending its information feelers out into the world via massive underwater cables. There was also an ample supply of green energy, thanks to the island's thermal power plants. We had already seen a number of things happen that one would previously have only thought possible in novels. So why not give our freedom-of-the-media idea a shot?

At a pre-interview breakfast, Egill Helgason, a veteran TV

presenter, did a double take, his coffee cup suspended halfway to his mouth, when Julian proposed the idea. I saw a gleam in Helgason's eyes. I knew that meant we would be able to propose the suggestion on his Sunday talk show.

On the way back to our small corner room with its floral pattern curtains, beige plastic wastebasket, and toilet down the hall, we jabbered away, full of self-confidence. We were to mix up Icelandic politics a bit. Wouldn't it be a gas if we could lead this likable little island out of its current crisis? Our next adventure was about to commence!

On the Sunday in question, a driver picked us up at our guesthouse and drove us out to the station, which was located atop a small hill just outside the city. Reykjavík was a bizarre place, both magical and inhospitable. The landscape was covered with snow and ice, and a cutting wind was blowing. The snowflakes that came flying at the windshield made it seem as if we weren't moving a meter. It probably wasn't much colder than it was in Germany, but I could have stayed inside that car forever. The world outside looked like the Antarctic. The sun dragged itself above the horizon, shone for a few scant hours a day, and then sank back out of view, exhausted. I felt tired all day and a bit depressed. As much as Iceland quickly won a place in my heart, I could almost have suspected that it wasn't only going to bring me good. Maybe I should have foreseen that there would be trouble with Julian, should we ever return here for an extended period. I had noticed a change between us that was increasingly giving me food for thought. Julian seemed unduly irritated with everything I said. Sometimes he didn't answer my questions, as if I weren't even there. Or he'd correct my choice of words like a pedantic schoolteacher. I hated the pedantry. He was a native speaker of English. Of course he expressed himself better than I did. I had to speak a foreign language the entire time—and even give interviews in it. But that wasn't the real problem. We were fighting about superficialities to avoid having to address the true conflict.

Something was wrong with my eyes. My eyelids felt far too heavy. I scanned people's faces for signs that my face looked strange. I was also constantly running to the supermarket to buy fresh orange juice. I think it was my way of combating light deprivation. Pictured on the bottles of orange juice I bought every day was a friendly, glowing orange ball that looked a bit like the absent sun. It made me feel as though even if I couldn't see the sun, I could still drink it.

Despite my sun-deprived fatigue, the talk show was a huge success. Helgason, with his blond locks, asked all the right questions, and after talking about WL and the Kaupthing Bank, we outlined our proposal to turn Iceland into a data haven. After our appearance on TV, the entire island knew who we were.

People would say hello on the street, give us hugs in the supermarket, and buy us drinks in bars. It was crazy. We were stars. I was almost ashamed at how much I enjoyed it. To play the hero for once felt good—I'd be lying if I said I didn't feel that way. In the beginning, we had to try so hard just to introduce people to WL. Journalists wouldn't return our calls for weeks. We held lectures attended by only a handful of people. We had been called rats, weirdos, and criminals. Now, for the first time, people simply loved us for our work. I was on cloud nine. I didn't notice any change in Julian. He assumed he would be treated like royalty, and took extreme care that he was the recipient of a few additional hymns whenever people sang our praises.

A WL trip was anything but a normal vacation taken by a couple of friends. We never cooked or watched a movie together. When we didn't skip breakfast entirely, we sat at the table with our laptops, taking bites from our rolls and typing in silence. We weren't far from me asking Julian via chat to pass the coffee. One time, however, we did go out in the evening to a club. There, too, everyone wanted to buy us drinks, to party and dance with us.

Julian and I weren't club-goers at all. In all the time we'd known each other, we'd gone out maybe fifteen times together. I remember one evening at a club in a former slaughterhouse in Wiesbaden. The others we were with nicknamed Julian "Disco King" or something like that for his unusual way of dancing. Julian took up a lot of space when he danced—almost like a tribesman performing some ritual. He'd spread his arms and gallop across the dance floor, taking huge steps. He didn't look very rhythmic or coordinated, and he didn't seem to have that much feeling for the music, but he did possess a certain cool. He didn't care anyway what other people thought of him. You need space, he once told me, if you want your ego to flow. That statement fit well with his dance style.

During the day, we mostly hung around on the sofas in Café Rot, a cozy little restaurant run by squatters in a house that had been scheduled for demolition. On Sunday, people danced to swing music, and the coffee only cost one euro. Refills were free, and you could work there the whole day.

• • •

Three days after our club outing was the FSFI conference, and that's where we met Birgitta Jónsdóttir. She was a member of the Icelandic parliament and wanted to become informed about the data-haven idea. Birgitta belonged to the Movement—a new party that had been voted into parliament in the wake of the financial crisis and with the support of protesting citizens. She was a poet, and more a freethinker than a politician. She was also a big fan of Tibet, had taken part in countless demonstrations, and had traveled the world. After our lecture, she came up to us and we went for something to eat. The fact that she was a parliamentarian immediately awakened Julian's interest.

Julian could turn very polite whenever he thought he was in the presence of someone important. He shook Birgitta's hand, bent forward slightly to ask her name again, and tried to pronounce it correctly after she had repeated it. Icelandic names were a nightmare for someone like him. He turned Birgitta into Brigitta, and that was the way it stayed, even though she accompanied us for months and soon became one of our closest confidantes.

In Iceland, I also got a tattoo. I liked tattoos, and I was always in search of images with a special personal connection. New tattoos for me were mementos of special places that I could take back home. Iceland was one such special place.

I mulled over for a long time what I wanted for an image. The idea to have the WL hourglass tattooed on my back was one I'd been carrying around with me for a while. I remember that I told Julian about it and he thought it was great. Later he always made fun of me, saying he found the idea pathetic.

Some people from Karamba, a café where I sometimes drank Americanos while I worked, recommended the Icelandic Tattoo

Corp. The tattoo studio was concealed behind a milk-glass window on a main road, and as I pushed open the door, causing a bell to ring, there was a young man in the place who spoke German. When I asked for an appointment, he just shook his head. No chance, not for months. He laughed as though I had asked him whether he believed in Santa Claus.

I was about to turn around and go, when a second tattoo artist stuck his head out of a back room and recognized me.

"Hey! I've seen you on TV, and I like what you do," he said.

Smiling, he approached me. We shook hands, and he said his name was Fjölnir. I showed him my image. He said he'd do it right then and there.

Unfortunately, the tattoo only got half finished. Both the tattoo artist and I were too exhausted after four hours to press on. I needed two Tylenol with water and was constantly asking Fjölnir which country of the logo he was on.

"Now doing Iceland."

I sighed

"Morocco."

Oh my God.

By the time we got to Cape Hope, hope was something I no longer had. We decided to adjourn the session.

As a result, to this day I run around with half of a WL logo tattooed on my back. And that's how it's going to stay. It's appropriate to me and my story—today even more so than back then.

On one of our last days in Reykjavík—we were sitting in Café Rot—I grabbed Julian and we went for a walk. I wanted to talk to him. We set off toward the harbor, the snow falling on our winter hats.

I wanted to find out what was wrong between us. I could only guess what was bothering him. Recently, he had become very concerned that he get at least 52 percent of the attention and me only 48 percent. Maybe he felt as though someone was now there with whom he would have to share. Someone who was grabbing his laurels, someone who also wanted to be praised and who was developing his own ideas about how to proceed with WL in the future. It was easy sharing a lack of success. But he was unwilling to allow our success to be credited to both of us. I tried to take account of and pacify his feelings. For me it was clear that he had founded WikiLeaks, and that no one was going to take away his baby. On the other hand, I was part of our success. I did my work well, and there was no reason for me not to say that.

I returned to the guesthouse feeling as though our conversation had done us good. As I brushed the snow from my clothes in the entrance, I thought that maybe we'd just been under too much stress the past few weeks. Everything, I thought, would now go back to the way it had been before.

10

Going Offline

JULIAN and I were the sole representatives of WL to the outside world, but our pretense of having a robust team in the background wasn't a complete lie. By 2009, we already had two silent partners, in addition to our occasional helpers. We called them "the technician" and "the architect."

There were two reasons for the secrecy surrounding this pair of collaborators. Neither of them particularly wanted to be identified as a WL principal. They were reticent types of guys. And truth be told, it was probably more important to protect them than to protect Julian or me. Slowly but surely, they had taken over responsibility for all our technology. If our adversaries wanted to do permanent damage to WL, they would have been best advised to go after one of them and coax out their secrets.

The most noticeable thing about both of these technical specialists was how inconspicuous they were. It wouldn't be easy to describe them so that someone could pick them out of a group of twenty people. Techie number one had been with us since 2008. He was the first to arrive, which was why he was simply called the technician. It's hard to say exactly when he started at

WL. Cautious as we were about new people, Julian to the point of paranoia, they were gradually accepted into the project, step-by-step. The technician was relatively young, but that wasn't a problem. We could both see that he was a solid, reliable worker. He was a quick study, and when we gave him something to do, he always did a good job. He wasn't interested in getting involved in our internal affairs. It was almost embarrassing for him when he witnessed one of our quarrels or we asked him for his opinion.

The technician felt more at home in an all-weather jacket and hiking boots than in the aggressive attire of the IT scene. He was haggard and often looked a bit pale, and he talked very quietly. I know little about his private life. Did he have a girlfriend? I have no idea. Someone called him constantly when we were at HAR, but he never answered the calls. He just looked at the display and put his phone aside.

The hackers' conference in Vierhouten was a really big deal for him. It took him a while to feel at ease, but after he had observed the proceedings for a couple of days from his chair, he began to get to know some of the others. Soon he was gleefully swapping action films.

Strangely enough, he subsisted exclusively on yogurt. One time, at HAR, I wanted to do something nice for him and returned from the supermarket with a broad assortment of yogurts. He wouldn't touch most of them. He only wanted the ones from Danone. I pray for him that he'll live to see a ripe old age.

The architect, as we called our second technician and in-house genius, got fully onboard with WL early in 2009. He came via a distant contact of mine. He had been volunteering his services for a while, and in late 2008, we gave him his first concrete task.

Within a couple of hours, he had carried out an urgently needed modification of our system, delivering a perfect, elegant solution. I'm not a particularly gifted programmer myself, but I can see when someone has done his job well. And the architect was brilliant. Extremely quick and extremely smart, he was never satisfied with anything less than perfection. To my mind, he's one of the best programmers in the world. In addition, he's also a good designer.

Julian kept the architect waiting for a number of weeks, refusing to implement his solution. That's a true test of patience for a programmer of this person's quality. Any company boss with half a brain would have immediately offered him a steady job at a top salary. It was a miracle that the architect stuck with us. That was due in part to my powers of persuasion. It pained Julian deep in his soul to allow anyone else access to the server. The very thought made him squirm. In fact, he had never given our other technician full access, something that often made the technician's job unnecessarily difficult.

The architect couldn't believe his eyes when he was finally allowed a look at our system. Amid all the threats and little fights that would later envelop WL, the real scandal in the eyes of the architect was the jungle of extraneous lines in our programs and the dilapidated state of our infrastructure. What he saw was a chaos of insufficient resources and overly vulnerable, dilletantishly improvised stuff that showed no sign of clearly defined processes or proper workflows. The architect got down to work.

The first thing he did was to establish clear roles. The two technicians would standardize the formats and forward the material on to us. The division of labor was now clear: The technician and the architect took care of the technology; Julian and I, the content. When everything was cleaned up, we sent servers to various parts of the world, using standard mail delivery. Volunteer helpers received them and arranged for the hosting. That was their way of making a donation. So finally our resources were divided up between various legal jurisdictions, and we concealed the network that connected the various servers. In a commercial company, you could have assigned a whole team, working full-time, to this mess for half a year, but the architect was even more diligent than we were. By a long shot.

What was the architect's motivation? What drove him on and sucked him in? I think he was intrigued by his job for its own sake. What we had built up was, from a technical standpoint, unlike anything else in the world. This was pioneering work, a new frontier. It offered him the chance to become the Columbus of whistle-blower platforms, the Thomas Edison of submission architecture. The project was challenging in a host of ways related to both the architecture and the underlying structural considerations. Then there were the security aspects and the whole range of legal constructions. Our servers were located in countries with the most favorable laws and the best protection of sources.

The architect had no more desire to grab the spotlight than the young technician. But he did have strong opinions, and he made no bones about them. People who didn't know him found his tone difficult to get used to. He had no time for polite phrases and friendly clichés. Whatever he said was extremely short and to-the-point. He never accepted half-truths or well-intentioned reassurances. An answer like "Just trust me" made his blood boil. "That means either someone doesn't have a clue or he's trying to fuck me over," he once remarked. The architect demanded arguments, not rhetoric.

Later on, when major conflicts broke out within the team, emotions came to a head, and mutual accusations took on irrational proportions, the architect was always the voice of reason. I think he felt his primary loyalty lay with the idea of WikiLeaks, not with any one person, including Julian or me. He is a truly independent spirit, bound only to the quality of his work. But because he also applied the same high standards to his own behavior, you could always rely on him. Even though we quarreled a lot, I always knew he wouldn't react irrationally, play with loaded dice, or follow a secret agenda of his own. He was entirely devoid of avarice, envy, and cowardice.

Throughout 2009, the two technicians, Julian, and I had given everything we had. But by year's end, eleven months after I had quit my job, our war chest was emptier than ever before. The publication of the material from September 11, 2001, had exhausted our resources. The 500,000 text messages had created a minor media hype, and our website almost collapsed under the demand of people wanting to view them. Processing the messages, putting them in the form of easily readable documents, was also a huge amount of work.

We had decided not to publish all the messages at once but to release them gradually so as to mirror the sequence of events on the day of the attacks. The idea was to re-create the passage of time realistically and not swamp readers with masses of information. That also had the indirect advantage of allowing us to better manage requests for access to our site—or so we'd hoped.

The WikiLeaks.org page was still run from a single, battle-worn computer. For the text messages, we had created a specially dedicated website, which was run simultaneously via various servers. This was only possible thanks to volunteers who provided capacity and placed their servers at our disposal. Even still, our infrastructure was bursting at every seam. For a year, we had been running around trying to repair everything ourselves. But as soon as we fixed one thing, something else would break. The hard drive was constantly full of newly received documents, hardware had to be replaced, and we had massive problems with our operating system, which was in dire need of an update. We didn't know where to start. The architect was working day and night on a general overhaul. The system had grown enormously over the years, and the program code was a tangle of Dada-istic formations. No one had an overview anymore. Least of all Julian. For quite some time, he'd felt no need to bother himself with technical details.

Our decision to go offline was unanimous. We wanted to send a message to the world. If you want us to continue, you've got to give us a bit of support. It was like a kind of strike. Our stance was nonnegotiable. We took the site offline on December 23, 2009. For the first time in a long while, we finally had some peace and quiet. And it felt good, admitting that things simply could not continue the way they had.

For two years, an invisible force had drawn me to my computer, sucking me into the chat room or onto the Internet. Every day, some new problem would arise, and there was never time to take a breather. Shortly before Christmas, WL having released me from its clutches, the feeling was unbelievable. I regained my sense of perspective. It was relaxing. But also somewhat unaccustomed. Something was definitely missing.

I drove to see my family. I put my feet up and did nothing but eat and unpack presents. I spent time again with my girlfriend. When we had seen each other in the months before, which wasn't all that often, she always said I did little more than take up space with her. I would work, and she would sit behind me on the bed, her legs crossed, and look on in concern over my shoulder. At some point she'd say, "I'm going to sleep."

I'd keep on working. "Do that," I'd say.

She'd wait half an hour and then get up slowly, come to me at my desk, kiss me from behind on the cheek, and go to bed. I would hardly react. I'd just tilt my desktop lamp down to the floor a bit and keep on working.

I felt no desire to fall asleep at her side. I would climb into bed in the wee hours of the night and instantly plunge into a deep slumber. I had nothing to complain about actually. The only thing that plagued me was a bad conscience, and it was gradually getting worse. She must have felt pushed to one side.

Then in December 2009 came the 26th Chaos Communication Congress (26C3). The congress was always the highlight of the year for me, but this time around—there's no other way to put it—it was the ultimate mood enhancer. I suddenly knew what it must feel like to get endorphins injected directly into your brain.

Julian and I were the keynote speakers, the main event in the best time slot in the middle of the day. To accommodate everyone who wanted to hear us, they would have had to install another floor halfway up the walls.

We had distributed pieces of paper with numbers on them to the audience. I then told them that we'd been approached in Iceland by the "Christmas Gang," who had given us a leak: a leak of all the people who probably weren't going to get any Christmas presents next year because they hadn't done their duty toward society. Everyone with a number had a year's time to fulfill his obligations. In return, we'd put in a good word for them with Santa Claus. In the months to come, we were constantly receiving donations and offers of help connected with these numbers.

Next we gave our audience an account of Iceland, our idea for setting up a safe haven for the press there, and the appearance on Egill Helgason's talk show, where we had made our proposal public. Then we asked an open question: Were those in the audience at the bcc capable of truly comprehending why the freedom of the Internet was so vital?

It was the greatest moment of my entire life. We hadn't given a pop concert or promised to hand out a thousand free drinks. All we'd done was give a lecture about international media law. But people clapped like crazy. First one member of the audience, then two, then three stood up, and suddenly they were giving us a standing ovation. The noise was deafening. I felt waves of enthusiasm floating up to us like a cloud from the masses down below. That was an awesome feeling. Truly awesome.

Slowly but surely, money started coming in.

We had announced that we needed $200,000 for operating

costs and, ideally, $400,000 more for salaries. By February or March 2010, we had gotten the first $200,000 together, and that was just in our account with the Wau Holland Foundation, which ran our German account for us. This had been set up in October 2009. The Chaos Computer Club had put me in touch with the foundation, which was named after the deceased information philosopher. Holland was one of the founding fathers of the CCC, and the foundation managed his estate and supported projects that furthered freedom of information. The good thing about the foundation was that it took care of the donations and ensured that everything went through official channels. Anyone in Germany who wanted to give us money could deduct it from his taxes. I made contact and took over the paperwork. The lion's share of our donations came from Germany.

In the first two weeks after our initial post-strike publication, the "Collateral Murder" video, we raised another $100,000. By summer 2010, it was already $600,000, and the last time I was able to check, the foundation had collected as much as a million dollars for us. When I left the project in September, we had invested $75,000 in hardware and travel costs. In the following two months, a far greater sum was withdrawn—probably because a way had been found to pay salaries.

With the submission system sorted out, we went back online in January 2010 so that people could upload new documents. The background system was, technically speaking, far more advanced than it had been before our break, but the wiki—the user interface with the start page, the explanations of all the leaks, and the links to the documents—remained offline for another six months. For half a year, we could receive new material but were otherwise unreachable via the Internet. That was because our repair operations had proved a bit trickier than we originally imagined.

Suddenly there was plenty of money available, and unlike Julian, I was in favor of spending it. Between March and May, for instance, we got some seventeen new servers up and running.

Transactions with the foundation were relatively simple. The foundation advanced me money, and I bought things and submitted the receipts. Once I received 10,000 euros, and later, on another occasion, 20,000, which went to buy hardware and pay for transportation and travel costs. In late August we updated our infrastructure again. When I left WL in September 2010, the project was in the sort of technological shape I'd always dreamed of. We had Cryptophones, satellite pagers, and state-of-the-art servers—everything we needed. We were on solid footing, and our architecture was exemplary.

We also needed an office and some permanent employees. We'd been talking about this for some time. As a headquarters, we'd considered Berlin or somewhere in the Alps. Julian enjoyed the fresh air and the mountains just as much as I did.

In 2009, we briefly toyed with the idea of getting an air-raid shelter. I went as far as to ask the German military if there were any unused sites for rent or sale. The plan was to set up a computer center, which could have also served as home for related projects by other people we wanted to support. We would have hoisted a giant WL flag above it. It would have underscored our reputation as an unassailable fortress. Our stated goal at this point was to become "the most aggressive press organization in the world."

Then suddenly, as money began pouring in, Julian changed his mind. He thought we should become an "insurgent operation."

Insurgents? Insurgents don't have offices. They work under-ground. To my mind, he was casting doubt upon the basic idea of everything we'd worked toward for years.

Increasingly, he would talk about how we were being shad-owed and how we needed to make ourselves "untouchable." He was convinced we were no longer safe on the streets, that our mail and belongings were being searched, and that we had to disappear and live underground. He fantasized about bulletproof vests and international secret services always on our heels.

Now, I'm a big critic of the German government, but I still believe we live under a government that respects the law. I didn't think we needed to fear being kidnapped on our trips to Iceland, Italy, or Hungary. And before we started complaining about peo-ple breaking into and searching our office, it would have been nice to have one.

Our first truly serious fights were about the money. I explained to Julian that he wouldn't be the only one to have access to the funds from the Wau Holland Foundation. I wasn't interested in paying them out to myself. I just wanted to be able to make deci-sions. To be able to get money when it was acutely necessary and when Julian, as was often the case, couldn't be contacted for a couple of days. Our two technicians and the close circle of assis-tants that had coalesced within WL shared my view. They even suggested splitting the money into two halves so that no one could squander it all individually. Even if one of us made an awful decision, our war chest as a whole would have been safe.

We all worked full-time for WikiLeaks. We had talked about the need to pay salaries for quite some time. I would have been content with 2,500 euros a month gross. I didn't need anything.

What's more, the foundation had told us that any salaries shouldn't be too nominal, to avoid running afoul of German labor laws concerning who was a freelancer and who a permanent employee. That was fine by me. We had talked about modeling what we did on the practices of other charitable organizations such as Greenpeace or Worldwatch. But Julian blocked any and all changes. There was more money around than ever before, but precisely at this juncture arguments broke out about every cent. Such quarrels were unworthy of the project. The fundamental underlying question was much larger. Gradually I realized that we were heading toward a major problem. A true nightmare. The future direction of WikiLeaks was at stake.

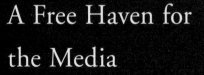

A Free Haven for
the Media

A T the beginning of January 2010, after our spectacular appearance at the 26C3, Julian and I flew back to Iceland to work on the IMMI—the Icelandic Modern Media Initiative—aimed to get the island nation to enact the strongest media-protection laws in the world. We had already announced the idea, of course; now it was time to help ensure it became a reality. We had generously allotted two weeks of our time for this task. Three, if need be.

In Germany, we had just helped derail the Access Impediment Law from the Ministry of Family Affairs headed by Ursula von der Leyen. Germany's president, Horst Köhler, had refused to sign the legislation into law. Now it was also time to get a law of our own through the Icelandic parliament. We figured we would run into some difficulties, but none that would prove insurmountable. In fact, it would be six months until German parliamentarians would even vote on our application for a resolution.

We rented an apartment in the Fosshotel, a half-decent chain hotel that would normally have been far beyond our means. But Julian, using various obscure connections, had gotten us an obscenely cheap deal. In the end we would only pay a nominal sum for a whole month. Julian paid the bill, which allowed him to play the generous host toward the rest of us.

Julian took the inconspicuous young guy who worked nights behind the reception desk into his confidence, telling him what we were up to, what an exclusive club he was dealing with, and how dangerous it all was. The bellhop became one of the gang. When we came home late in the evening from our discussions and meetings, he would shoot us a conspiratorial glance. He probably spent the whole night watching the hotel parking lot outside the glass entrance, waiting for the black CIA limousines to arrive.

So there we were, in a somewhat spartanly furnished apartment for four on the third floor, with a kitchen, purple curtains, and imitation-wood floors. The hotel with its massive, ugly, gray exterior was located on a quiet side street near the harbor promenade. The room I shared with Julian had only a single small window at about the height of my navel. But the view of Faxaflói Bay was still marvelous. I used to lie in bed and look out at the clean lines of the mountain panorama across the water, when the close confines and permanent mess of our quarters got to be too much for me.

But there was no window in our bathroom. In the morning, after the three other guys had taken their showers, the air was full of sulfuric water that bit at my lungs.

Julian and I shared the room in succession with Rop Gong-grijp; the American hacker and Net activist Jacob Appelbaum; and Folkert, a hacker from Hong Kong who was a good friend of mine. They had all come to Iceland to support the IMMI, bringing their experience and expertise and helping us work out the details of the idea.

We also met up practically every day with the Icelandic parliamentarian Birgitta, Herbert, and Smári. They all lived in Reykjavík. In addition, we received a visit from Harald Schumann, a journalist from the *Tagesspiegel* newspaper in Berlin, who was writing a story about us.

Birgitta, who was to get increasingly involved in WL, soon became more than just our main connection to the Icelandic parliament. As we soon noticed, she had little in common with the typical politician—the contrast between her and Ursula von der Leyen could hardly have been greater. She looked like one of us, always casually dressed in a long black coat. On the one hand she wore steel-toe boots, but she also favored feminine details like a silver chain, a blouse, or a floral hair clasp. Birgitta became the main mover of the IMMI. She had a different perspective on things and her opinions helped us a lot. She was a cool, immensely likable woman.

Birgitta put us in contact with lawyers who were likewise enthusiastic about our ideas for bolstering Icelandic freedom of the media. That surprised me. The lawyers then set about fine-tuning the legal framework for the IMMI.

We rented a workspace in the Ministry of Ideas—an old warehouse complex in Reykjavík that is home to a number of grassroots movements. Space was cheap there. The Ministry itself was a large echoing space with a gray stone floor. The table and chairs looked as though they had been borrowed from a school classroom. There was a small coffee bar, and we commandeered one of the couches in the back to hold discussions and bat around ideas for the IMMI.

When I wasn't sitting at my computer, I was meeting potential business partners. The idea was to convince the service providers, regulatory government offices, computer centers, and the companies who owned the transatlantic cables that it was in their interest to support our initiative. If they could guarantee people legal protection for all Internet business, I argued, they would attract customers from all over the world.

Two of Iceland's advantages were green energy and a cool climate. There was no question that the country was an excellent location for servers. Nonetheless, that alone was no way of achieving our stated goal of increasing data transfers by 30,000 percent. In fact it would have exceeded the capacity of the newly laid transatlantic cables!

What is much more important than green energy for providers and customers is legal protection. Knowing they would no longer have to deal with criminal censure and that they wouldn't have to face incalculable legal costs was an advantage that greatly outweighed any certificates of environmental friendliness. In return, we argued, that would create jobs and bring money into the bankrupt country.

Icelandic regulators feared that our idea would create wrangling with other countries over competition and legal issues, and that they might attract unwanted illegal exchange platforms and the porn industry. Their worries, though, were unfounded. The IMMI was directed chiefly at the media, and it was nothing but bringing together already existing freedom-of-information laws from all parts of the world—the best of the best.

Our first priority was to find a date when the proposed legislation could be brought before parliament for discussion. A preliminary hearing was arranged, and with considerable effort, we had come up with a presentation. Even if I now say I can be woken up out of a deep sleep and still improvise an acceptable lecture about WL, the IMMI was virgin territory. Just like anyone else, we had to think through all the legal and political implications, and what's more, we didn't have much experience with the Icelandic political system. Overnight, we had to become experts.

Our appearance before Iceland's parliament—the Althingi—in Reykjavík was an extremely unhappy experience. Our presentation was scheduled for a Tuesday afternoon, and we pictured ourselves captivating at least half of the members of parliament with our performance and turning them into fervent IMMI supporters. At that point, only Birgitta and two or three other politicians were onboard. Birgitta had taken the lead and was drumming up considerable noise for the IMMI, trying to elicit nonpartisan support for the initiative. But we didn't know how many people she'd succeeded in winning over.

On our way to the conference room at the Althingi, I was astonished at how quiet things were in the hallways. I was accustomed to far more activity in the German Bundestag.

We got a slap in the face when we entered the presentation room. There were only two parliamentarians seated in the ten rows of chairs. The rest of the chairs were empty, and the room was silent save for a draft blowing through an open window and rustling a couple of papers. The majority of the politicians, we learned later, were either on vacation or visiting their local constituencies.

We began the presentation. It had taken hours, if not days, just to plan who would say what and when. Julian spoke first and he didn't allow himself to stray from his agenda. Nor did any of the others. When it was my turn, I shortened my planned script. The situation was so absurd. At lectures with more speakers than listeners, form no longer matters. You might as well have a good old-fashioned discussion. This was all the more true since the two parliamentarians in attendance, as we soon learned, didn't need to be convinced.

If Julian was upset, he didn't show it. Shortly after the lecture, he whisked himself away to the Ministry or perhaps somewhere else. I was a bit depressed. How were we supposed to make the IMMI into Icelandic law if only two people attended the pre-liminary hearing. Two parliamentarians plus Birgitta. We still needed sixty more to achieve our aims. And we'd already spent three weeks in Iceland.

It then occurred to me that we were no longer accustomed to setbacks. I'd almost forgotten what a sparsely filled auditorium looked like or how it felt to speak to an empty room. I don't know why we thought everything would take care of itself. In addition to all the appointments we had, the IMMI formalities were eating up a lot of time. The home page for the initiative had to be completed, a logo designed, and a layout developed. Texts needed to be written, and positions discussed. We'd gotten a bit distracted and underestimated the amount of work involved.

The next major obstacle took shape invisibly and came from our own ranks. Along with piles of dirty clothes and empty pizza boxes, cabin fever was beginning to take over our apartment at the Fosshotel. Although we all got along extremely well and worked together very efficiently in chats, none of us could stand the physical presence of others for so many days in a row. It was almost funny. Everywhere in the world the IT branch is accused of creating problems between people by keeping them apart. Video conferences and electronic meetings replaced face-to-face talks, detractors often argued, and people had to over-come feelings of distance and misunderstanding that could have been easily cleared up if they sat down together. With us, the exact opposite was the case. Our first serious clash of personalities probably never would have happened if we hadn't rented a shared apartment in that Icelandic hotel. Or at least if we had each had a room of our own.

On a Wednesday evening during the third week, the situa-tion escalated dramatically. The cause was an open window. I had been out and about and had returned to the apartment, where everyone else—Rop and Julian as well as Herbert and Smári—was hunched over his laptop, typing away. A coffin that had been reopened after a decade would have smelled better than our room. I held my nose, went over to the French balcony on the other side of the room, and opened it to let in a bit of oxygen. Herbert shot me a grateful look. He had already retreated once to the hall-way because he found the air unbearable. Julian, however, froze in front of his computer, only raising his head to fire a question at me. What was I thinking, opening the window? There was fire in his eyes, and it was directed at me.

"Rop is cold, you idiot," he said in an extremely insulting tone.

I had no idea why he felt he had to play the role of Rop's father. The others looked at Julian and me in horror. Rop had in fact said he was cold, but I didn't intend to leave the window open all night. I said as much. Julian didn't respond. He just stared at me, leaving no doubt that he expected more.

I went back and shut the window, perhaps louder than needed. Then I left the room.

That evening made clear how quickly the mood could turn sour.

I bought some swimming trunks and goggles and submerged myself in the warm water of a nearby outdoor public pool. It was nice only to perceive the outside world—the cries of children, the blubbering of water pumps, the smacking sound of flip-flops approaching and then receding again on the edge of the pool—in muffled, distant form.

In Iceland, people go to outdoor pools even when temperatures are freezing. There's no need to worry about heating costs. Volcanic springs bring bath-temperature water to the surface of the earth. The atmosphere of the dark, evaporating water at sundown and the view to the right and left of the snow-covered peaks were almost mystical.

All around the pool, in the changing rooms, the showers, and even in the toilets, there were signs with every sort of instruction imaginable. DON'T DIVE FROM THE POOL EDGE. DON'T SWIM ON A FULL STOMACH. CAUTION: SLIPPERY. PLEASE KEEP THINGS TIDY. NAKED SHOWERS REQUIRED BEFORE SWIMMING. Sometimes the other guys—chiefly Rop and Folkert—came along with me, and we'd start messing about with ideas. Rop suggested that we start a campaign demanding safety for everything. We should insist that the entire world be plastered with signs and stickers for even the minutest detail. The politicians would be completely swamped with this task, rocked to their foundations. It would be a particularly congenial way of creating anarchy.

We had a lot of crazy ideas like this. One was buying a boat, preferably one capable of laying cable on the seabed, and traveling the world in a floating office. Another was getting money together for a tour bus and cruising through Europe in the first-ever bookmobile for secret documents.

Without our noticing, four weeks had passed. We weren't making progress with the IMMI, and the question was what were we doing there? I asked it. And that didn't make me very popular.

"What about WL?" I wanted to know. We'd already abandoned our work for a month. Our submission platform was filling up with new documents that had to be reviewed and prepared for publication. "When are we going to continue?" I asked.

I had seen our task as being to get the legislation going. Now it could take care of itself. There were Icelanders, after all, who were looking after that.

"Why isn't that enough?" I asked.

But Julian couldn't, or didn't, want to let it go. He considered the IMMI his baby. Later, he made undiplomatic statements that damaged the whole project politically.

None of us were simple people. And as the pressure mounted, our personal relationships showed the first cracks, especially the relationship between Julian and me. The others were more like film extras helplessly watching our fights. Toward the end of our weeks in Iceland, Julian accused me of losing perspective, of getting distracted by the minor details and losing sight of the bigger picture. I can't remember any one decisive incident. Nor can I recall what prompted our first major quarrels. Probably it was banalities like open windows.

I began to criticize Julian's appearance. For example, I told him he should generally pay more attention to how he looked. He was very insulted. But do you have to meet with the Minister of Justice looking like a bum?

We also had a very unpleasant discussion about who was senior and who was junior in our ranks. Julian set up a pecking order of who was allowed to criticize whom, with himself at the apex of the pyramid. That was justified by his intelligence and experience. But because at the time he was somewhat closer to Birgitta, he also decreed that not only he, but she as well, was exempt from my criticism. The latter, he said, was tantamount to criticizing him.

At one point, he said he needed to have a word. Birgitta, he informed me, was getting completely irritated with me. Later I asked her about this, and she just laughed, saying there was nothing to it.

"Everyone here thinks you're being unbearable," he said.

"Who's everyone?" I asked.

"Everyone," he said. "Anyone who has to deal with you."

Julian apparently didn't like us sharing thoughts among ourselves. He said that if we started discussing things on our own, the truth would become "asymmetrical." In Iceland, he was in danger of not being able to keep track of everything as he could in the chat room. He was worried that the others might go out for a coffee and simply start talking.

. . .

In no time, the Fosshotel apartment looked like an asylum for psychotic slobs. At the start, the cleaning women had still been able to plow a path with their large black vacuum cleaners through our things, but soon they couldn't even get the tools of their trade through the door. For a few days, these friendly Icelandic ladies battled to save apartment number 23. But after five days at the most, they surrendered the terrain as lost. We agreed to an armistice and began swapping shopping bags full of trash for fresh towels and toilet paper.

None of us cooked or even bought anything sensible to eat. Half-empty bags of potato chips began to collect amid our dirty laundry. A pile of stinky dried fish that someone had bought but no one thought was edible lay rotting away on some surface. Things were getting worse by the hour. We should have patented the smell of old socks, pizza crusts, dried fish, and sulfur as a means of torture.

I need at least a modicum of orderliness, the faintest hope of keeping an overview. I can't concentrate with total chaos around me. I could drink as much orange juice as I wanted from the bottles with their bright sunny faces, but at some point, my head began to spin, and twenty laps in the outdoor pool wasn't going to make it stop.

The apartment was way too small for us, especially since Julian was always occupying himself with one woman after another.

One night I really needed to sleep. I was dead tired, and I asked him to just let me crash in peace for once. A short time later, I heard Julian talking to a woman on the phone. He laughed into the mouthpiece, and I could tell she had just said that they could meet at her place. I sighed to myself. But Julian insisted she come to the hotel. My problem was that we shared not only a room but a large double bed. I buried my head in my pillow and tried to sleep, or at least give that impression.

There were also fights because he constantly made others wait. Coordinating a large group of fairly anarchic people is difficult enough as it is, requiring a positive desire for organization. But no matter whether we had an appointment or just wanted to go get something to eat, everyone else would usually be standing in the doorway, ready to roll, while Julian had to be asked for the umpteenth time to tear himself away from his laptop. I was the only one who had a serious word about this with him and who got irritated if he kept typing. The others preferred to wait stoically until he got himself together.

I was in bad shape. The stress, the worries, and the aggravation had shredded my nerves, and I could no longer calm down, even for a moment. Iceland was a lovely place. Later, I returned there with my family for a vacation. But something in the apartment, in the air, in the sulfuric water, in the lack of sunlight, in the chaos, and in Julian's bossy manner was making me sick.

Before I completely lost my shit, I booked a flight home on February 5.

"I'm taking off the day after tomorrow," I told him. "I can't stand it anymore."

We weren't parting on friendly terms.

It would be the last time we would ever see each other in person. Our communication was once again restricted exclusively to the chat room.

12

Back to Berlin

I TOOK the subway directly from the airport into the middle of Berlin and parked myself on a couch at the Chaos Computer Club. I often spent the night there when I was in the German capital.

I was feeling pretty down. Perhaps if I had known that a few hours later I would meet the woman who was to become my wife, it would have cheered me up. The nice thing about my life is that misery and joy often come in quick succession. But without that bit of advance knowledge, I shuffled my way through the club building, totally dejected. It wasn't much sunnier in Germany than in Iceland, and when others asked me how things had gone in Iceland with the IMMI, I waved them off. "I'm too tired," I said. They left me alone. Thankfully, despite the solidarity that club members feel for one another, the chance that they would pester you and ask you tons of questions was relatively small.

I took a walk in search of some food. Although I rarely smoke pot, I rolled myself a joint and tried to relax. Almost accidentally, I arrived at Dada Falafel, a trendy, fast-food kiosk on one of Berlin's most popular tourist streets. Even more accidentally, I met someone I knew there, in the company of a woman.

My friend introduced us. "This is Daniel, Mr. WikiLeaks in Germany." He pointed to me. "And this is Anke. She works for Microsoft." He pointed to the woman who would become my wife and added, "She's really nice."

I bit into my falafel and took stock of Anke through coleslaw and hummus. Cool woman. Fashionably dressed but with a style of her own. Very confident. With a good sense of humor.

We ended up talking the entire evening while everything around us faded into the background and our food grew cold and then congealed on our plates. At some point, someone cleared the table. They could have replaced the entire interior, set off fireworks under our feet, or handed out hundred-dollar bills, and we still wouldn't have noticed. We were completely lost in our conversation.

Back then Anke had barely heard of WikiLeaks. She knew next to nothing about Julian and me. She worked for Microsoft on open government projects. In principle, she was trying to increase transparency from the top down, while we were working from the bottom up. I thought she was probably very good at her job.

Anke was constantly on Twitter, describing everything that happened to her. That very evening, she tweeted that she had met "one of the WL founders" in Dada Falafel, and that we'd had a very interesting talk.

Around one-thirty in the morning, I returned to the club. My head was buzzing with thoughts, some about the past, others about the future. I stayed awake for a long time, and it was a nice feeling to get into my sleeping bag. It was my sleeping bag and my sofa. At long last I was alone again at night. And for the first time in quite a while, I was thinking about a woman. I wondered whether Anke liked me. Bizarre. I couldn't help shaking my head. Where had my bad mood gone? I nestled into my pillows and dozed off. I bet I was smiling as I slept.

From that point on, I met up with Anke almost every day and quickly recovered from the cabin fever of Reykjavík. So I was in high spirits when I got back in touch with Julian for the first time in four days. I told him what a find Anke was. His first reaction was "Make sure you dig up some dirt on her." I'd need it later, he said, when things went belly-up between us. Then I'd have something on her that I could use. I was dumbfounded. But Anke just laughed when I showed her the chat.

"Hey, I'm sorry things were so difficult with me the past few days," I wrote back. I've never had a problem apologizing, and this time it was even easier than usual. Back in Berlin, I could see that I had in fact come off the rails a bit in Iceland. When I pictured myself in the hallway of the Fosshotel, nervously tapping my foot and feeling like I was going to explode just because Julian had again made us wait for five minutes, the Daniel in Iceland seemed like my evil twin. An intolerable bundle of nerves. Realizing this actually calmed me down. It would have been far worse if all of Julian's accusations had been completely invented.

I desperately wanted everything to be right. I didn't think at the time that his judgment about me would be permanent.

I asked him what he blamed me for, what had gone wrong, and why he suddenly no longer wanted to work with me. He only gave one-sentence answers.

"We can't go into that now," he wrote.

"Later?" I asked.

"Maybe," he wrote.

If there's one thing in this world that's dead certain to unleash a bout of rage in Julian, it's when he reads in an article that "Daniel Schmitt" is a cofounder of WikiLeaks. "Founder"—the word was like showing red to a bull. He was always afraid that I would claim that title. Ever since WL really began to take off and attract money, attention, and even celebrity, he apparently felt as if he—the person who had conceived, nurtured, and defended everything—was having to share his fame with some vagabond con man from Wiesbaden.

I knew the feeling of not having my own performance and ideas sufficiently recognized, and I tried to understand Julian's concerns. But the more I thought about it, the less I could.

In fact I had been well trained always to mention in conversations with journalists that I was an early participant in, but not a founder of, WikiLeaks. I'd bring it up even when no one asked me. Sometimes before I had even taken a seat. Even now, months later, I ask journalists just to make sure whether I ever claimed to be a founder of WL. I always said I "got in early and stuck around."

When I told Julian about Anke, he immediately asked if she was the one who had met the "WL founder." The idea that I was using his WL to get women must have kept him awake at night. He probably imagined me hogging the conversation at the kiosk, surrounded by ten supermodels to whom I related one boastful WL story after another and who ultimately threw themselves at my feet.

Anyway, in my opinion, no one cared as much about who was a "founder" as the founder himself. Most journalists weren't interested in the topic at all. I could have told them I was Deputy Press Spokesman for Special Questions: Germany and Central Europe—they had to write something.

Julian even told me that my friends at the computer club were whispering about me. It got to the point where I didn't even invite some of them to my wedding. Julian said that people there had advised him to get rid of me because my work with the press in Germany was so lousy. Or that I held people back from getting involved with WL because they didn't identify with me and my anarchic view of the world. I was very sensitive on this score.

Julian accused me of being most afraid that someone from the club would take away my job. That was a misapprehension. What actually bothered me most was that someone might be maneuvering behind my back, not the desire to remain the WL spokesman at all costs and some fear of competition. It would have really disturbed me if the solidarity within the club had disintegrated. Suddenly I was forced to ask myself how well I knew the others.

For a long time, I hadn't been a Chaos Computer Club member and hadn't paid any dues, but I had tried to show my gratitude in other ways. I procured hardware, helped out at events, and assisted in setting them up. I was never much for club board meetings and stuff like that. Nonetheless, I felt a bit guilty toward the club because I'd slept so often on their red sofa when I was in Berlin. I asked others how they saw things. They said, "You've been part of the club for a long while now." That was a great honor. It was almost as if I'd been knighted.

The club had already been through its fair share of hassles, and

I wasn't the first one who had attracted a bit of attention for what it did. A lot of club members before me have achieved far more than I have, and one person's success can always lead to jealousy among others. That happens in the best associations. But the club had managed to survive any personal conflicts and remain intact. One important factor, I think, is that no one there is truly jealous or resentful of anyone else's success. The only reaction is curiosity. People ask if they can help. On the other hand, everyone basically sticks to his own business. It took months for me to contact the people Julian claimed had been talking behind my back and ask them if we could clear up any problems.

A further bit of nonsense of this kind was that I was on the verge of being recruited by a state intelligence service. People like me, who are under a lot of stress, can easily fall victim to offers of that nature. The only thing is, I've never received one. I ask myself which secret service would have been interested in me and what sort of tip-top job they were supposed to have offered. Canteen cook? Archivist for secret documents? The conspiracy theories sounded like they had been taken from a bad secret-agent novel.

Shortly after I flew back to Germany from Iceland, Julian began attacking the Icelandic political system and the Ministry of Justice in particular, even though we were supposed to be working with them to make the IMMI legally airtight.

The Twitter account had originally been conceived as a neutral channel for us to inform our followers about news and fresh articles about WL. We also alerted readers to articles critical of us, in keeping with our basic philosophy. But the account quickly developed into a channel for whatever Julian Assange happened to be thinking at any given moment. At some point, he began talking about "his followers" and "his account." Under no circumstances was anyone permitted to criticize his tweets. One minute he would insult some journalists, calling them total idiots; another he would tell a mailing list of 350,000 people he had no time for interviews.

One time, he issued a tweet attacking a journalist who worked for the American investigative magazine *Mother Jones*. Later, at the WL press conference on the Afghanistan leaks, the journalist in question used the opportunity to ask what had been so bad about his article. Julian answered something along the lines of "I don't have any time to take apart that piece of shit." He continually went on about how journalists didn't work objectively or base their pieces on primary sources, as should be part of any serious approach to reporting. But he himself never provided any proof when people asked him for evidence for his various tales of persecution.

I never understood why Julian was so obsessed with the idea he was being followed. It was almost as though he could only be convinced of the significance of his own opposition to the status quo if people thought of him as public enemy number one. In Iceland, he once bought a Solzhenitsyn book titled *First Circle*. He found the volume in an antique bookshop, and discovering it put a broad smile on his face. Solzhenitsyn is a must-read author for the leftist, anarchistic scene, but for Julian, the Russian author had a special significance. Julian identified with the dissident writer, who was imprisoned for many years in a Soviet gulag and was later exiled to the wilderness of Kazakhstan.

Julian saw a number of similarities between his own biography and that of the trained mathematician and philosopher.

Solzhenitsyn, who would go on to win the Nobel Prize for Literature, was arrested and interned for criticizing Stalin in letters written to a friend. In an early blog entry, Julian had written that "the moment of truth" only arrives "when they come to take you away." This entry, titled "Jackboots" and written in 2006, is an example of Julian's tendency to engage in heroic romanticism. In it, Julian wrote about how similar the experiences made by scientists in Russian work camps were to events from his own life. True commitment could only be attained when they come to get you, "when they kick down your door with their jackboots." Oh boy! Maybe he thought that anything less dramatic simply wouldn't do.

On numerous occasions, Julian accused the Icelandic police of keeping him under surveillance. He also informed our—no, sorry, *his*—Twitter followers that two operatives from the American State Department had followed him onto a plane while he was en route to a conference in Oslo. Our hotel, too, had been watched, Julian trumpeted, and unmarked cars had tailed us. He loved these stories because they assured him of a rapt audience. Once, he terrified a woman he was spending the night with so much with his secret-agent stories that she fled and was too scared to return to her own apartment. Julian stayed behind and made himself comfortable.

The rumors that he was being followed originated in part from his overactive imagination. But they also had the advantage of giving him the aura of someone in dire peril, increasing the collective anticipation of every new leak. Julian didn't need a marketing department. Marketing was something he himself knew best.

13

Collateral Murder

JULIAN and the others began to work on the "Collateral Murder" video while still in Iceland. Involved were Birgitta, Rop, and two or three Icelanders who primarily did technical work. Our techies and I worked from home. The others rented an old house on the outskirts of Reykjavík. There they sequestered themselves, drawing the curtains and preparing the video for release.

Two of our collaborators got promoted to regular members of the WikiLeaks team during this phase: the Icelandic journalists-filmmakers Kristinn Hrafnsson and Ingi Ragnar Ingason. It was undoubtedly due to their influence that our next release would be more journalistic than any of those previous. Both came from television, and they convinced Julian to process the video material like a documentary film.

Kristinn quickly understood what WL could mean for him personally as a journalist. Today, he is WL's new spokesman. I think he brought along Ingi and later the seventeen-year-old guy who would eventually become something like Julian's personal assistant. Exactly what he was never became clear to me. Julian called upon Kristinn in many of the later accusations he made against me. "Kristinn can confirm that you stirred up the others, Kristinn this, Kristinn that."

We had a tacit agreement at this point that I would not be returning to Iceland. I didn't ask to come back, and I sensed that Julian didn't want me around. It was no problem for me to work for WL from Berlin, and I had good reason for wanting to stay in the German capital: Anke.

Julian and I never resolved how things would continue between us. I tried to engage him in a discussion, but he steadfastly refused. We only ever communicated in the chat room, although a lot of people were saying that we simply should have gotten together and repaired our relationship.

Our chat conversations were getting more and more bizarre. In May, I made another one of my many attempts to clear the air with Julian.

> D: i need to understand what we can do to get back to a level of mutual trust j
>
> D: whenever you have a minute to talk about this, let me know
>
> D: just need a constructive conversation
>
> J: i don't know where to start. and if I had to explain it, what would be the point?
>
> D: the point would be that we want to keep going?
>
> D: and i still think i am one of the few persons you can trust, like really trust
>
> D: and there are not too many of these around
>
> D: for what the last 3 years have been worth, it should be worth it

J: pathological liars always have great faith in their own honnesty, that is what helps them lie

D: why do you think i am a liar?

D: i cant recall i ever lied to you, ever

D: i feel like you are listening to lies others tell

D: and dont even bother to ask me about it

D: i on such a fundamental level dont get why you would think i am a liar

D: boy, thats so way beyond what i even imagined

J: you have fucked up in so many ways and you want me to enumerate them. but what is the point if you can't see things things for yourself?

J: I want you to work it out yourself.

D: because i challenge that list

D: i cant work it out myself, because at least half of it is not even true

D: its stuff that has never happened and you think it did

D: so how would i be able to work it out?

J: These are direct observations. Not 3rd hand information.

D: then i get it even less

J: I already gave you a giant list of why I was pissed off at you six weeks ago.

D: that list that included that my suit is well pressed most of the time?

D: i really dont get it

    The list. My God, that was truly insane. Julian had made
me a list of what he felt had been my many shortcomings in the

preceding months. One of them was the perfectly ironed pleats on my suit pants. We got dressed up perhaps once every three months. We had some public appointments where I was convinced we could achieve more in conservative attire than in the normal slacker stuff we wore. Solid in appearance, subversive in performance, that was my motto.

Julian, by the way, also started wearing suits far more frequently in his later public appearances. Perfectly ironed suits. I found that appropriate. There's a great quote from Daniel Ellsberg, the famous whistle-blower who in 1971 leaked secret Pentagon documents on the Vietnam War to the media: "I always like to wear a suit when I think I'm going to be arrested, because it shows that even men in suits aren't above the law."

Julian also took exception to the fact that my name was now on the doorbell of Anke's apartment. I always asked myself why he got so worked up about that. He said I was endangering my own security. But I always had my name on the doorbell, even before moving into Anke's apartment. That was the case in Wiesbaden, and Julian had lived with me there for two months. Whenever I moved, I also replaced the locks, buying new and more secure ones. It wasn't easy to break into my apartment. Any lock can be picked, of course, but I'd taken care that if someone did invade my space, I would know about it.

I had recently bought a year-long rail pass that allowed me to go wherever I wanted by train. The money for the pass, 3,800 euros, came from the sum that had accumulated at the Wau Holland Foundation. I could just get onboard, and there were no credit-card transactions to betray where I was at any given time. I was safer than ever before.

It had been a long time since Julian had had a permanent residence. He'd move here and there, always finding a place to crash.

What is also probably true is that he and his mother moved around a lot during his childhood, never staying anywhere for long, always fleeing her boyfriend, who was a member of an Australian New Age sect.

I had experienced for myself for much of 2009 how it feels to be without a home. I had given up my apartment in Wiesbaden in July 2009 and hadn't had a permanent place to live for seven months, right up until I moved in with Anke. In the beginning, I might have thought it would be interesting to share Julian's lifestyle, and it was an interesting feeling to be without any ballast. But by "in the beginning" I mean only the first month.

I quickly grew to hate not having a home. I missed my kitchen the most—a place where my food, spices, and groceries were, where my sense of organization ruled and where I could cook whenever I was hungry. I had stored my things—two vanloads full, one for my kitchen appliances and one for my hardware—with my parents. My plan was to retrieve my possessions once I had found a place in Berlin. I was always on the go with a giant backpack, staying in cheap guesthouses during conferences or just crashing with friends. But I couldn't find an apartment, because I never had time to look for one.

Then I met Anke. It took around a week for it to become clear that I was moving in with her. I think that when she later saw the red sofa I slept on at the computer club, she was glad she had taken me in. Her apartment was spacious and comfortable. There was a cuddly corner of cushions in the living room, and her kitchen was a gift from heaven to my starved, nomadic soul. It's possible that Julian was a far greater nomad, and that this didn't bother him. But my time on the sofa at the club made me sympathetic to anyone who wanted a home.

I also became a father. My new stepson was named Jacob, and he was ten. We actually got along perfectly, right from the start. From my new home base, I resumed working for WL with a second wind.

At first, things calmed down in the chat room. The others seemed to have so much to do with the video that they had no time. But then the first debates erupted—chiefly about media strategies and donations.

Julian would later claim that the work on "Collateral Murder" had cost $50,000 and say that he wanted to recoup that sum in donations. He also asserted that a lot of the work had gone into decrypting the videos. I knew for a fact that this was not entirely true. We did occasionally receive encrypted videos, but with this one, we had the password. The resolution only had to be augmented to improve the video quality, and that was done mostly by volunteers. In essence, Julian's only costs would have been rent for the house in Iceland and the price of his plane ticket. Others provided the capacity for the servers free of charge.

Julian sent Ingi and Kristinn to Iraq to talk to eyewitnesses and do background research. They later contacted me, while I was on a private vacation in Iceland, and asked me to reimburse the cost of their flights to Baghdad. They had paid for them themselves, and Julian had promised to refund the costs. But he turned around and told them they just should set up their own foundation in Iceland. He said it would be child's play to earn back the money. Apparently Julian had discovered that WL was a fantastic business model, capable of earning large sums of money. I asked the Wau Holland Foundation to reimburse the two Icelanders for their flights and gave them the money.

In conjunction with the "Collateral Murder" video, the question of rights arose for the first time. TV stations were calling us to ask if they could use the video, whether a higher-resolution version was available, and how much it would cost. We agreed that they should make a donation or, if their statutes prohibited such contributions, pay us a fee for being interviewed.

The issue of getting money in return for the video left a bad taste in my mouth, and I wasn't the only one who felt that way. But Julian always cut off any discussions between me and the others. "Do not challenge leadership in times of crisis," was one of his favorite answers to any critical questions we asked.

Together with Rop, Julian flew to Washington to hold a press conference in the National Press Club about the "Collateral Murder" video. Before the flight, he took his leave from us in the chat room with the words: "I'm off to end a war."

A short time later, there was some talk about WikiLeaks being awarded the Nobel Peace Prize. The architect told me that Julian had mentioned this to him. I was amazed. Then the same message came in from Julian himself. "There's a chance we're getting the Nobel Peace Prize." I subsequently did in fact discover a message in our in-box from a Swedish supporter, who wrote that he knew two university professors who were allowed to nominate people for the Nobel Prize. He could ask them if they thought WL deserved to be on the list of nominees. But, of course, we weren't really about to follow in the footsteps of Dr. Martin Luther King, Mother Teresa, and Barack Obama.

From Berlin, I had taken care of the invitations, the space, and the live stream for the Washington press conference about the "Collateral Murder" video. When the chips were down, we still worked well as a team. Or to put the matter the other way around: three days before the event, nothing in Washington had been organized in any serious way. If I hadn't taken care of the details, Julian would have had to address the journalists in the hallway of the National Press Club. Or in front of the building. That is, if anyone knew that the press conference was being held at all.

When Anke and I decided to get married, Julian was the first person I told. That was in March 2010. Julian and I may have been going through a difficult phase, but he was still one of the most important people in the world to me. After Anke and I had set a date, I told him I'd be really glad if he would come. He never answered. We were fighting at the time about money and the future direction of WL, and some hard words had been exchanged in the chat room. Afterward, I never mentioned the wedding. I didn't want to open myself up to the disappointment of his saying no. In fact, there was nothing I wanted more than to have Julian there.

On the eve of the wedding, he then kicked up a huge fuss about how I hadn't invited him. Meanwhile, he was the very first person I invited! "I never received a written invitation," he complained. "Where the hell was I supposed to send it?" I replied. What's more, we had decided against printed invitations anyway.

· · ·

On April 5, "Collateral Murder" went online. It was viewed more than ten million times on YouTube alone. It is shot from the gun turret of a military helicopter and shows American soldiers killing Iraqi civilians. Two Reuters journalists also died in the gunfire. The video was our definitive breakthrough. Afterward, just about everyone knew our website. Reuters had for years tried to get the video. Outrage was the response around the world at the soldiers' cynical comments as they shot at civilians who rushed to help the two journalists and the other victims in a small bus that had been driving by. Outrage, and a more realistic picture of what was supposedly a "clean" war.

"Collateral Murder" might have been a good title in a literary sense. But we also got a lot of criticism for it. We had given up our position of neutrality. By cutting together our own video from the raw material and subtitling the soldiers' comments and radio transmissions, we were ourselves manipulating public opinion. But what caused the most umbrage was the title of the video and the quote from George Orwell on the page: "Political language is designed to make lies sound truthful and murder respectable, and to give an appearance of solidity to pure wind."

The questions people raised were precisely the ones that we had always discussed among ourselves: How much did we have to process the material to ensure it would have an effect? Were accusations of partiality an acceptable price to pay for attracting such huge public attention to a leak? What could we leave to journalists, and what should we be doing ourselves? We had put a bit of distance between the website with the processed video and WikiLeaks to indicate that this was not original source material. We had created a separate domain, CollateralMurder.com, where the video was posted, and then linked it to WL. One thing is clear: in their raw form, the film sequences would have had far less of an effect.

Nonetheless, in my view, this strategy for stirring up public interest was a mistake. A lot of people immediately watched the video only to feel, when they examined it more closely, that they were being led around by the nose.

We were always experimenting with our role. We constantly made mistakes and tried to learn from them. But as long as you admit your mistakes, I think that's all right.

14

The Ordeal of
Private Manning

THE next lesson we were forced to learn was a very hard one indeed. In May 2010, the American intelligence analyst and private first-class Bradley Manning was arrested. In a chat, someone whom American authorities believed to be Manning had told the former hacker Adrian Lamo that he had passed on confidential military documents to us. Among the material that this person had allegedly copied from US military servers were the sequences we had used for our "Collateral Murder" video and the cables sent by US diplomats.

We learned of Manning's arrest from the news. I was sitting at my computer when the first reports came through on online media. It was the worst moment in the history of WikiLeaks.

Manning, who was formerly stationed in Iraq, was sent to an American jail, and according to a report by Glenn Greenwald in *Salon* magazine in December 2010, he hasn't been treated particularly well. He allegedly sleeps without a pillow or a blanket, is subject to round-the-clock surveillance, and spends twenty-three hours a day in solitary confinement. He's purportedly not even allowed to do simple exercises like push-ups—a guard personally assigned to him ensures that he doesn't break any of the rules.

At least one American Congressman, Mike Rogers (R-MI), has called for Manning to face the death penalty, and prosecutors have demanded that he be sentenced to no fewer than fifty-three years' imprisonment. We realized immediately that the US government was not going to let the opportunity pass to make an example of someone. From that point forward, anyone who considered passing on material to us would think of Manning and the potential consequences the young soldier was facing.

When we learned of Manning's situation, we let it be known that we would support him in any way possible—be it by providing money and legal representation or by mobilizing publicity on his behalf. None of these offers confirmed in any way whether Manning was, in fact, our source.

We ourselves actively did not want to know who our sources were—that was part of the WikiLeaks security concept. All we asked from our whistle-blowers was a reason why they thought their material was worth publishing. Their rationales varied in the extreme. Whistle-blowers could be frustrated employees, unsuccessful job applicants, or individuals motivated solely by moral concerns. The spectrum was broad. We wanted to prevent our platform from being misused for personal acts of revenge. Protecting our informants, though, was our top priority. At least, we *aimed* to protect them. Whether in retrospect we did everything correctly was another issue. And we couldn't necessarily protect them from themselves.

For the first time, we were seeing the social shortcomings of our project. No matter how well prepared we were for various crisis scenarios or how much we always talked about security measures, be they Cryptophones or solid locks on our doors, we hadn't devoted enough attention to this topic. At WikiLeaks, recognition and risk were unequally distributed. While we basked relatively safely in the spotlight of public interest, our sources knew no fame and ran a far greater risk for doing what they did. WL depended on whistle-blowers secretly scanning or copying sensitive documents and sending them to our platform. Without their courage and the documents they secretly reproduced, we would not have been able to offer the public such unique views of what went on behind closed doors.

We considered a variety of technical solutions to the problem of unfairness. Perhaps we could give whistle-blowers a kind of token with a personal code: After all the statutes of limitations had expired, the source could then redeem the token for a premium. After twenty years, he could buy a T-shirt, a certificate, or—rather unconventionally—WL underpants he could wear unnoticed under his normal clothes.

We would also have liked to set up some sort of feedback system, a channel to communicate directly back with our sources. Of course, one basic idea of WL, and a main security guarantee WikiLeaks offers to informants, was that there's absolutely no way to find out who our sources were. On the other hand, it would have been helpful for journalists to be able to contact them. But that would have been going too far. If we had turned reporters loose on our sources, the latter wouldn't have been able to protect themselves at all. Based on my experience, I wouldn't advise any informant to contact the traditional media with a digital secret document, not even if that person had a personal contact or was offered a small financial reward for the material.

There had been one case comparable to Manning's in the past, although the material involved was not nearly as incendiary. It involved student fraternities. Fraternities had become something of a running joke for us since their secret ritual handbooks so regularly turned up on our submissions platform. We could have filled a whole set of shelves with books from fraternities. Kappa Sigma, Alpha Chi Sigma, Alpha Phi Alpha, Pi Kappa Alpha, Sigma Chi, Sigma Alpha Epsilon, Sigma Phi Epsilon—we had them all.

Among other things, these books contain the initiation rites used to torture new members—occasionally to death—and the secret codes, symbols, and songs of these groups. The scenarios described in their pages ranged from altars containing a skull-and-crossbones and a Bible to flags that had to be hung to the right and left of windows to a chemists' fraternity's demands that its pledges bring a long list of substances, presumably to be stolen from the lab, to their initiation for a bit of perilous magic. At the bottom of that list was a fire extinguisher.

We asked ourselves whether fraternities were important enough that their handbooks merited publishing. We decided in the end that every pledge had a right to know what he was letting himself in for, so we put all this nonsense online. And once we had published one handbook, we had to be consistent and post all the others as well.

These leaks earned us great animosity. Members of Alpha Gamma Whatever were always popping up in our chat room, and soon we felt like we could identify a frat boy from the first sentences he wrote. The message usually began: "Really awesome." Then a pause and: "I think it's totally great what you're doing." And then there'd be a sentence like "I've got a question about a publication. . . ." Sometimes, we'd answer directly: "Say, are you a member of a fraternity?"

That was fine until someone gave us a handbook that had been reproduced using a digital camera. These handbooks always have a number on the first page, telling you which university it's from, and at every university there's someone responsible for keeping the book secret. Our source had manipulated the photos to black out the telltale number, and we converted the files to PDFs and published them. But someone also uploaded the original photos onto a forum that was frequented by fraternity brothers. It wasn't hard to make out the number from the back of the first page. That revealed which university the book—and thus the source—had come from.

Fraternity members, upset at the betrayal of trust, began to scour pictures on university servers and college communities, comparing the metadata from them with the metadata from the photos of the handbook of rituals. As a result, they soon found out the owner of the camera and the presumed informant. Things could have gotten pretty bad for him.

Fraternities copyright everything, from all their songs on down to the last idiotic secret gesture or handshake. But not their secret rituals. That was fortunate for the person they accused of being the leak. Because fraternities were paranoid about someone finding out about this secret, they didn't even show their handbooks to a copyright office.

Our loyal chat guests were deeply unhappy that we were exposing their secret associations to public scrutiny. Once they'd realized that we weren't going to remove the books from our site, they reacted with rage and, more frequently, whining. Occasionally I used to discuss the matter with them. They argued that nothing was more important in their lives than their fraternity. Paternal advice from me, to the effect that they should wait ten years and they'd feel differently, did nothing to alleviate their sense of loss. Once their secret rituals and codes were on the Internet, they could no longer be sure who was and wasn't one of their fellow brothers. One of the main reasons for secrets is people's desire to share them only with a select circle and exclude everybody else. Fraternities are a very vivid example of this.

If it were true that a person like Bradley Manning was the one who uploaded the material we used to produce "Collateral Murder," I could understand why he had done so. Manning was in his midtwenties, a person sitting in Iraq, isolated from his normal social contacts and probably surrounded by soldiers who had completely different attitudes toward war from his. The person in question may well have felt the need to talk to someone about his experiences, and that could have been why he acquired the video material and documents.

It was probably impossible to expect people to keep knowledge like this to themselves. Probably most of our sources contacted us because they felt they simply had to share with others what they knew.

Working for WL taught me that secrets are almost never kept.

I wonder whether there even is such a thing as a secret between two people. I think they are very, very rare. If a sentence began with the words "I'll only tell you if you promise not to pass it on," it was nearly a foregone conclusion that this promise would get broken in another sentence beginning with those same words. This sort of prelude only prevents a secret from being spread quickly; despite what people may have promised, the secret would still make the rounds in the end. Even if someone's best friend or spouse were the one being told, the danger of revelation was there—at the latest when the two parties in question got into a fight.

Whoever copied the "Collateral Murder" and diplomatic cables material was running a huge risk, the dimensions of which may not have been clear to the whistle-blower himself. Perhaps he suspected that he was doing something forbidden, but he would not have known the extent of potential consequences. More than likely, the person in question was driven by moral considerations. But regardless of whom we have to thank for the material, any source should be told repeatedly not to talk about it with *anyone*. It would have been good if one of us had been able to offer this counsel to our sources.

However, the anonymity guaranteed by WikiLeaks's anonymizing mechanisms is the main advantage WL enjoys over all classical forms of investigative journalism. In most countries in the world, no journalist can guarantee a source, in any serious way, that his name is safe from the pressure and legal instruments of investigative authorities. The technical and legal construction of WikiLeaks, on the other hand, ensures whistle-blowers' anonymity.

But legal security is only one part of the story. In the course of our work, we repeatedly saw how naively most journalists handle technology and modern means of communication. Sensitive documents are anything but secure on the computer of the average reporter.

When was a document so dangerous that we could no longer publish it? We discussed the topic a lot, particularly in conjunction with the leaked diplomatic dispatches. After Manning's arrest, we posed the question somewhat differently: When was a document so dangerous for the *source* that we should no longer publish it?

Theoretically, the problem can arise with every publication. What were we supposed to do, for instance, when a source contacted us three days later and asked us to delete his documents? Should the source always have the final say?

That was precisely the question we faced once with a leak concerning Italy—one that ironically proved to be of little interest to anyone. The leak was about the questionable way in which a contract had been handed out, and the source contacted us a few days after we had published it and requested that we withdraw our allegations of corruption. I replaced the word "corruption" with a milder formulation in our summary of the document's content, but I didn't remove the document itself from the site. That wouldn't be easy, from a technical standpoint, if it is indeed even possible.

The result was a series of questions. How could we be sure that the source wasn't making a request for withdrawal because of external pressure? How could we be certain that, if we gave in, others sources wouldn't be put under similar pressure in the future? And how could we know if it even was the actual source who was making the request? We concluded it would be in everyone's interest to institute an ironclad policy of automatic publication after submission. As soon as anyone decided to upload documents on our site, he had decided they would be published. We had to draw the line somewhere.

In return, we constantly tried to devise ways of preventing innocent parties from being adversely affected. We aimed to consider every aspect that could be problematic for the real people named in the documents or for the source. Those aspects varied from case to case. For example, it meant that we sometimes deleted names—or at least addresses and telephone numbers. We weren't always as successful as we would have liked, though, and that was to become the biggest problem we would face with our Afghan war diary and Iraq war log leaks.

Nonetheless, it was important to send a signal that exerting pressure on sources was not going to yield the desired result. That no matter what happened, we were going to publish the material we received. I think, by and large, this was a sensible decision.

We had received the "Collateral Murder" material and diplomatic cables from someone—whoever that might have been—and we had already published the video. Manning was then arrested. Given the opaque nature of the situation, we should have ruled out any further publication of the American documents. Every new release risked providing further impetus for investigations of anyone suspected, rightly or wrongly, of being a source. I opposed further publication right from the start.

There are lots of myths surrounding what led to Manning's arrest. On the surface, the story was simple: He had chatted with

Adrian Lamo, and that was what set the investigations in motion. Still, anecdotes and conspiracy theories flourished. There were some indications from the United States that the "discoveries" made by American authorities might not have been as accidental as they initially appeared. At Defcon—a security conference for computer technology, held in Las Vegas—in 2010, there was a lecture about a government project called "Vigilant." According to the talk, security officials were involved in scanning the Internet broadly in search of relationships and data transfers that would reveal connections between people. If a lot of material was transferred between A and B, alarm bells would ring, and authorities would begin investigating. It's entirely possible that people who worked for the US Army snooped around on their own servers. That wasn't particularly problematic. Two million people in the United States alone had access to documents with the same level of secrecy as the cables. Intelligence services only got actively involved when material was obviously being passed outside that circle. And this, according to the story told at the conference, was how Manning had attracted their attention. Later, the US government would deny the whole strange tale.

But there are also other, even more obscure, theories concerning personal motivations. Lamo himself claims he turned Manning over because he recognized the global political importance of the material and felt morally compelled to act. Ultimately, the question is to what extent a chat can even serve as evidence. It's hard to identify people in chat rooms.

It's possible, though, that the whole story was much more banal. US authorities may have only decided, in retrospect, to present Lamo's accidental discovery as the intended result of their own investigations. That, in any case, would have been a logical move.

We will probably never know the whole truth. Proceedings in front of military tribunals aren't public, and those concerned will invest considerable energy to ensure no one smuggles any information out of these tribunals.

When people who obviously wanted to offer us material appeared in the WL chat room, they were usually directed to me. It was important to caution them not to reveal too much about themselves. We had a standard warning we constantly repeated: no names and no identifying information. We had to prevent people from writing things that would allow conclusions to be drawn about who they were. Our internal standards were quite high. After all, we subjected ourselves to the same restrictions on talking about material.

Julian had a fine nose for especially interesting material and how it could be used to exert political influence. Discerning what was truly interesting was something we had learned over the years, from negative experience as well as positive. There would occasionally be documents we believed would be of interest but that failed to create a stir.

One such example was a series of field manuals we received, including US Army handbooks on waging unconventional warfare. They described the methods used to weaken other countries from within and replace a head of state with a military regime. At the time, I thought this handbook would cause outrage around the world, and I expected journalists to beat down our doors. But no one cared, because the subject matter was too complex.

Videos were another thing entirely. Even if the images only related to one concrete incident, we soon realized how great an impact a video could have. Julian, in particular, developed a keen eye for this.

Julian was a hacker and the book he collaborated on, *Underground,* was highly regarded in the hacking scene. As much as he professed to despise hackers because they weren't politically motivated, he was not a complete stranger to the heroically clandestine nature of what they did. But at its core, WL functioned completely differently. WL was a platform, a tool, an instance of technology devoted to absolute neutrality, not intervention.

Julian's later accusations that I was typical "middle management" likely give an insight into his way of thinking. Despite the fact that we were equipped with Cryptophones and worked with the curtains drawn, and although Julian mentally transformed innocent plane passengers into State Department spies, we were all just administrators, managers, and press spokespeople—anything but true warriors of the digital underground. We were people who rented servers. We waited for material instead of soliciting, contracting, or hacking it ourselves. That was the way we understood our jobs, and regardless of whether Julian found it sexy, it was important for us to be like that.

It has been suggested that by posting our "Most Wanted" list WL was, in effect, soliciting material from its sources. This practice was patterned after the one from the Center for Democracy and Technology, on our site. It was intended to appeal to our potential sources' sense of adventure, but it also pushed the boundaries of intervention. It must be said, however, that we hadn't drawn up the list ourselves but rather asked our readers to make suggestions.

Externally, we made it known that we, of course, would do everything in our power to support Manning without implying in any way that he had anything to do with the leaks. Julian announced that he was going to organize top lawyers and unleash a giant wave of media interest. He called for donations, saying $100,000 was needed to provide Manning with the best legal help. I arranged the server where the Support Manning campaign would run. Someone else was supposed to be responsible for the content.

But early on, the initiative was already stalling. When I asked Julian about contacting Manning's attorneys, I received no concrete answers. Journalists were constantly calling me, and their questions were persistent. The Association of German Scientists had gotten in touch, with the idea of awarding Manning their whistle-blower prize.

I inquired about this with Julian, but his answer was:

J: i have no time to explain that and given you don't need to know it; next...

J: i know why you were asking which makes it all the more infuriating

D: so why am i asking?

J: some moronic disinformation campaign

D: no. i am asking because i am putting my ass out there on the line for an official position that you have claimed, and that i get asked about

J: lawyers names can't be given. they're not our
   lawyers names to give. They're bradley's lawyers,
   blah lbah

J: you don't need to know because you can't tell people,
   bah blah, hence waste of time

I have to admit that we at WL, myself included, utterly failed on this score. Unfortunately, as was too often the case, I simply yielded to whatever Julian said. I complained often enough about Julian being a dictator who decided everything on his own and withheld information from me, and I wouldn't take back that criticism. But that didn't absolve me of responsibility. I shouldn't have let myself be worn down by the stress. I should have asked more questions and taken the initiative myself, if necessary. There was no reason why Julian alone should have been responsible for us supporting Manning.

In the end, we took part in the campaign, organized by family and friends, that ran on the Bradley Manning Support Network. Later, we argued about how much we should actually contribute. Julian thought the $100,000 we'd asked our supporters to donate for his cause was too high a sum, and revised it downward to $50,000. As of this writing, $15,100 has been transferred from the Wau Holland Foundation to the Bradley Manning Support Network.

15

The Afghan War Diary
and the Dead-Man Switch

WE had tried out a number of variations with leaks. We had simply loaded them onto the site without any fanfare; we had gotten individual journalists onboard; and we had held press conferences as a media organization. But in the summer of 2010, we were determined to do everything right. We were sitting on a huge pile of documents concerning the war in Afghanistan: 91,000 of them, to be precise, from the US Central Command. The Afghan War Diaries, as they were known, covered everything from status reports to information about firefights and air raids, details about suspicious incidents and so-called threat reports, and the procedures followed by American troops in combating insurgents. No newspaper, book, or documentary film had ever contained such profound and comprehensive firsthand insights into the war. It was simply fantastic.

We decided to get the media involved right from the start but remain in control of decision making. So we looked around for reliable partners. We soon decided on the *New York Times.* For strategic reasons, we wanted an American publication on our side,

and why not start with who we considered to be the most prominent and influential? Our second major partner was Britain's
Guardian newspaper, at which Julian claimed to have good contacts. In Germany, we decided to work together with *Der Spiegel,*
the country's most respected weekly newsmagazine. They were
my responsibility.

Marcel Rosenbach, Holger Stark, and John Goetz are three
experienced journalists who work in *Der Spiegel*'s Berlin office.
We had first really attracted their attention after the publication
of the "Collateral Murder" video and they had contacted us for
the first time at the Re:Publica 2010, a Berlin conference on the
Internet 2.0. I provided them with a completely encrypted laptop
so they could safely store the documents, and our media partners equipped them with Cryptophones. The irony was, we never
spoke on the phone.

We met once a week to keep one another up to speed and
ensure that everything was going well. We had agreed on a date,
July 26, 2010, on which both they and WL would simultaneously
publish the material. That date was still several weeks away.

The journalists went through the material and did their own
original research. We made sure that the documents would be
processed technically in preparation for the story as a whole to go
online. But the first problem had already cropped up.

We wanted to cooperate with a number of media outlets and
let more than just those three publications in on what we had.
But journalists are like dogs jealously guarding a bone when they

think someone is trying to take a story away from them. The publications we already had onboard all wanted exclusive rights to stories.

Marc Thörner, for example, was a German journalist who has written extensively and excellently about Afghanistan. He reported from the country for a long time, and his book *The Afghanistan Code* was widely praised by the press. We wanted to involve him in the background research and allow him, too, to view the documents. But the other publications turned up their noses. Some fly-by-night freelancer was being cut in on the deal? Large news publications could never allow something like that to happen. In their eyes, they played in a whole different league. Thörner, who would later write the most thorough report on the subject, would only be allowed to publish a day after the "big three." Although we had begun by saying we would never give up our ultimate authority over the details of how and with whom we cooperated, the freelance journalist was pushed to the side.

For me, Thörner was nonnegotiable, and I had said so to *Der Spiegel,* but the *Guardian* and the *Times* piled on additional pressure. Julian guaranteed them exclusivity. As confrontational as he often behaved toward us, he was completely tame with the journalists from those two newspapers. I know, of course, that it's difficult to get your way with the media, and there was no doubt that these guys had more experience than we did. What had we been thinking? Getting exclusive, hot news was their stock in trade. We should have known that they would try to impose their rules on us.

Our original plan was to get everyone together in London. There, they would lock themselves in a basement somewhere and confer about the material—similar to the procedure used for the "Collateral Murder" video. We had agreed not to reveal to the journalists that even more revelations were waiting in the wings. In addition to the 91,000 documents, some other equally controversial material had arrived. Time constraints had only allowed us to a take a general look at it. But we suspected that we were sitting on a powder keg.

Nothing worked out as planned. Julian flew to London by himself, refusing offers of assistance from me and the others on our core team. I later heard that our colleague from the *New York Times* made it known immediately that he wanted to work in his own home office and took off back to the Big Apple as soon as he had copied the documents onto his laptop. Even documents about the Iraq War, which had never been part of the deal, ended up on his hard drive. Then he hopped a plane. That violated all the agreements we had made, but Julian permitted it.

David Leigh from the *Guardian* took over the job of coordinating. The guys from *Der Spiegel* told me that Julian often appeared at meetings looking completely exhausted or immediately submerged himself in work on his computer. Soon, it became clear that we were no longer in control of the process. We were completely swamped by the task of technically processing the documents. Our technicians were working round the clock to put the documents into a readable format.

The date of publication was set for a Monday so that *Der Spiegel,* as a weekly magazine, could stick to its normal schedule. In return, the magazine departed from some of its usual practices.

Parliamentarians in Berlin would not receive their usual advance copy on Sunday, and the electronic version would be delayed until we had gone online.

On the Wednesday before publication, I met Rosenbach and Goetz for lunch in an Italian restaurant in central Berlin. I wasn't very hungry. The menu was far too selective for my tastes, but to be polite, I ordered a bowl of pasta. While the other two talked, I twirled the noodles around my fork. The two journalists said everything was going swimmingly. I watched the ball of spaghetti around my fork getting larger.

"And you guys?" Goetz asked. "Everything going all right with you?"

I took a bite and nodded. The *Spiegel* journalists looked happy. Goetz was rubbing his hands. I got a bad feeling. I completely lost my appetite, though, when they asked me how far we had gotten with the "harm-minimization" process.

"Have you finished the blackouts?" he asked.

I stared into space like an idiot, fighting to keep my facial expression under control. They had agreed with Julian, Rosenbach reminded me, that we would black out all the names from the documents. That was a condition all three publications had set. It was essential before the material could go online.

I didn't know anything about it. It sounded logical to delete the names of innocent parties, and I didn't have any personal objections to it. But during this phase, Julian only ever told me crucial details very late in the game. That often put me in a difficult position with journalists. It was entirely possible that this was the explanation this time as well. I hurried home.

I immediately contacted our technicians and their assistants. They were all drowning in work. It was the first any of them had ever heard about blacking out names. We were caught between a rock and a hard place. The reports were as good as done, and the printing presses were already warming up. It was too late to stop production. It would have cost *Der Spiegel,* as a magazine, untold thousands of euros to cancel a publication date planned so far in advance.

I logged onto the chat room. Julian was there.

"Hey, what's all this about harm minimization?" I asked.

In an instant, he was gone. He didn't reappear for the rest of the day.

For everyone else, things were coming to a head. We did everything within the realm of possibility. I think that from that Wednesday to the following Monday I got only twelve hours of sleep, if that. Anke was living with a ghost.

A glance at the documents revealed that even when you blacked out all the names, enough contextual information remained to identify the people involved. If, for example, a report said that one of the three Afghans captured on March 25, 2009, in village X had turned informant, it would have been child's play for the local Taliban to find this person and exact retribution.

Ninety-one thousand documents! It was simply too much. I stared at my computer, at my wit's end. There was no way we could do what we needed to with the raw material. We required an Internet interface that would make the editorial omissions easier. Our technicians would subsequently develop a program with which large numbers of volunteer assistants could securely access the documents and black out the names that occurred there. But for our imminent publication, any such help would arrive too late. There was nothing we could do.

Thankfully, our media partners handed us a solution. They recommended that we sort out 14,000 of the documents and hold them back for the time being. The material in question was the so-called threat reports. They contained assessments of levels of risk based on warnings received from Afghans. If an Afghan knew about an insurgent attack and wanted to prevent it, for instance, he would get in touch with American troops. They would write up the information in a threat report, citing their source, making the informants easy prey for acts of Taliban retribution.

In the remaining 77,000 documents, names cropped up only very sporadically. Various people from the media later checked the documents and found only around one hundred names. A Pentagon spokesperson nonetheless said WL had "blood on its hands." It turned out that none of the informants were harmed by our publications. And it later emerged that the US Defense Department had concluded in an internal paper that the information we had leaked wasn't dangerous.

We were working as fast as we could go, when Julian turned up again in the chat room. He had been intending to tell us about blacking out names that evening, he wrote. He also presented us with a comprehensive to-do list:

> J: 1. the urls need to be standardized tomorrow. the
> naming has been standardized. "kabul war dairies"
> and "baghdad war dairies"

J: 2. afg needs to be checked for innocent informer identification. These are mostly in the threat reports. its quite a bit of work to go through them

J: 3. high level overview and press release need to be done

J: 3.5 our own itnernal coms must be standardized. sat pagers deployed if available and silc/irc fallbacks

J: 4. distribution infrastructure needs to be tested again

J: 5. versions of the afg database that we supply need to have the classification field stripped out

J: 6. i have made a full sql version of the database that also needs to be put up as one of the downloadable archives

J: 7. torrents seeded / archives pre-deployed

J: 8. email machines need to be made robust.

J: 9. press team / contacts standardized

J: that's it for the things that MUST be done or we fail

J: now for those things that need to be done if we are to do justice

J: 10. i have the perl based searchable/explorable front end i and the guardian developed. that also needs to be deployed as a downloadable archive [more on that later]

J: 11. a short 3 minute video intro needs to be made. I have people here ready for the film/editing part, but the graphics part (e.g. google earth / ground images) needs to be done

J: 12. the people [journalists] who worked on the data all need to be interviewed about their approach and the qua ities/limitations of the data. 10 to 20 mins each. no prep is needed. i have this assigned at the

> london end, but we also need to do berlin and new
> york. this is a fast way of producing a "guidebook"
> for the material, and also elevates WL into a clear
> working-in-partnership with these three major
> players
>
> J: 13. the press team needs to be robustified and we
> need a list of talking heads to can speak sensibily
> about the issues (not just us)
>
> J: 14. donation systems need to be checked / and made
> slightly clearer / the australian po box needs to
> be put up for cheques etc and possibly the .au bank
> account should also be expoed

I wrote back, putting into words what everyone was thinking: "It's only 4 days until the release . . ."

The hint about omitting the threat reports had come from our media partners. We hadn't had any chance to familiarize ourselves with the content of the documents. That was the journalists' job. Nonetheless, Julian would later get up in front of the cameras and rhapsodize about himself and his "harm-minimization" procedures.

Our technicians, too, put in hundreds of hours of work without ever getting thanked for it. For example, they converted everything into KML format so that WikiLeaks users could locate every individual incident on a timeline at Google Earth. Even without Julian's to-do list, the timing would have been incredibly tight.

Naturally, the night before we were scheduled to publish, we still weren't finished. The *Guardian* simply went online without us. The *New York Times* waited because they were afraid of being the only ones in the United States with the publication. And the people from *Der Spiegel* called me every hour, asking when we were finally going to put the leak on our site. It was utter chaos. But once the media machine had revved up, no one cared whether we had messed up the teamwork a bit and lagged behind our partners in publishing the material.

Around the world, there was a huge debate about whether this publication caused anyone any harm. There was less discussion of the actual content, aside from the first wave of coverage about the details and a second wave of analysis, once experts had digested the material. Julian had said that it was his mission to end a war. If he's succeeded, it's news to me.

We had expected the documents to change people's thinking about the war. If everyone could see how much wrong was being done in Afghanistan, we thought, people would protest and demand that their governments bring home the troops.

One problem was the sheer volume of data. The collection of material was too large for people to enter into the debate simply. And we still had 14,000 documents containing even more explosive stuff. Most of the reports published by *Der Spiegel,* the *Guardian,* and the *Times* were based on the latter. It was ultimately very much worth our three media partners' while to get to exploit this material exclusively, while the competition had to make do with the leftovers.

Naturally, it would be unfair to attack individual journalists for wanting exclusive access to good stories. I personally had good relationships with most of the reporters I knew. But the way the media functioned—the addiction to information possessed by no one else, the constant desire to squeeze as much as possible out of a story, the mix of permanent curiosity and friendly arrogance—disgusted me sometimes. I thought back to the days when we weren't so well known. When I had to contact the media to solicit their interest in good material. When they didn't call me back or answer my e-mails.

The majority of journalists viewed us with a critical eye during our first year of operation, and some wrote clever analyses of the problems our platform entailed. That was fine by me. Some of them changed their tune, however, when they realized how much attention our material could generate. They began to suck up to us. I found that quite strange.

Amid the debate engendered by the leaks around this time, criticism was growing ever louder that WL's only enemy was the United States. There were many corners of the globe, critics argued, that equally deserved to have the spotlight turned on them. And in fact, all of our major publications in 2010 were aimed at the one remaining superpower, the United States.

There were many reasons for this. First of all, Julian's frustration with American foreign policy was fed by the simple fact that the United States played a leading role in most of the world's major conflicts. Moreover, the suspicion could hardly be dismissed outright that the United States waged war partly for economic reasons. US intervention in the affairs of foreign countries was a particularly grievous sin. But one could have legitimately argued that it was equally important to criticize countries that committed crimes against their own people.

Another, more banal, reason why we focused on the United States was the language barrier. None of us spoke Hebrew or Korean. It wasn't easy to gauge the significance of a document even when it was written in English. Julian speaks no foreign

languages at all. Even though he exploited his advantage as the
only native English speaker among us in internal discussions and
diverted uncomfortable debates into pedantic lessons about the
precise meaning of this or that word, he himself was often unable
to remember the names of non-English media partners or collaborators. In a TV interview after I had left WL, he even tied himself
in knots trying to pronounce my real last name. We should have
tried to find more volunteers to help us with translations, but we
had already failed to integrate assistants for far more basic tasks.

The third and most significant reason for our focus, though,
was that by homing in on the United States, we were seeking
out the biggest possible adversary. Julian Assange had no time to
tussle with lightweights. He had to single out the most powerful
nation on earth. Your own stature, it has been written, can be
measured by that of your enemies. Why should he expend his
fighting energy in Africa or Mongolia and get into quarrels with
the Thai royal family? It would have been a far less attractive pros-
pect to end up in some jail in Africa, or wearing concrete boots at
the bottom of some Russian river, than to inform the world that
he was being pursued by the CIA. And it wouldn't have gotten
him on the nightly news.

The biggest problem we had in conjunction with the publication
of the Afghan War Logs was that Julian had gotten ahead of himself and showed the journalists our additional material. That tied
us to our existing partners. Our plan of remaining masters of our
own destiny had become a farce.

The *New York Times,* for instance, had cited WikiLeaks as the source of the leaked material, presumably out of concern that the link might bring them into conflict with the law. But they already had the material on Iraq. It would have been nearly impossible to stage the next link without them.

Some weeks after the Afghan War Logs leak, the *Washington Post* ran a long story titled "Top Secret America." It investigated the background of the military-industrial complex and convincingly illustrated how the sector had grown enormously as a result of the so-called War on Terror. The report was full of really good information. I don't know where it came from, but it was a true journalistic achievement. The piece also included numerous graphics and applications generated by the *Post*'s own editorial staff. People there had asked me whether they could have access to the remaining 14,000 documents. That would have been a sensible instance of cooperation. I would have liked to have rewarded their fine work with a part of our secret treasure.

Julian nixed the idea. We already had agreements with the other three periodicals, he told me, and there was no undermining them.

Today I think I made a mistake in not simply acting on my own. Categories like agreements and contracts meant little to Julian. He had told me on a number of occasions that the point was not to give in to other people's preconceived ideas but to take an active part in constructing the truth by creating facts. He himself would later break his promises of exclusivity with our media partners anyway, for instance, by giving the Afghanistan documents to Channel4, the British TV station.

On the other hand, I didn't want to damage WikiLeaks's reputation by making myself look unreliable in our partners' eyes. But I faced the double dilemma of someone who plays by the rules while having to work with someone else for whom rules were at most a rhetorical tool to be used when he saw fit.

Our own ideals of publishing material immediately and remaining independent in our decision making had become a joke. The media had us right where they wanted: WikiLeaks at their feet. They could market their exclusive stories while our hands were tied in terms of using the material as we would have liked.

Our technicians succeeded, within an amazingly short span of time, in creating a Web front end, a new user interface, so that volunteers could rid the remaining documents of compromising names. Every volunteer had access to a small package of work via the Web front end and only received an excerpt of the complete data. Hundreds of volunteers could view and edit the documents at the same time. There were at least two editors per document, and every change was protocolled. It worked like a charm. The volunteers were able to quickly redact the names from the remaining 14,000 documents.

The conflict between Julian and me continued to boil, even as we worked parallel to each other. Being fully in the dark as to what was going on in his head, I began to discuss our conflict in the chat room with Birgitta Jónsdóttir. As soon as Julian and I were on the same page, I thought, it would also be possible to put WL back on the right track.

In late June, Birgitta and I chatted about a conversation she'd had with Julian. She said that he had told her not to trust me and described me as his adversary.

> **D:** makes no sense
>
> **B:** no he thinks it is deeper. that you want to take over
>
> **D:** deeper in what way? thats BS [bullshit]
>
> **B:** money and credit
>
> **D:** yes, right, hahaha. well, this is clarified with everyone else. and we all agree on this being BS
>
> **B:** yes, good
>
> **D:** the only one that doesnt get it is J, will be sorted out sometime. i know why he thinks that way
>
> **B:** i hope so. why
>
> **D:** few remarks that i made for example. re money for example we had a discussion once about me spending some of that money
>
> **B:** he thinks you keep taking huge amounts of money
>
> **D:** and i said that if he doesnt talk to me, i will spend money for necessary expenses, in part because the money here in .de is in large parts a consequence of my work
>
> **D:** LOL [Laugh out Loud]. i took like 15-20k out of this account or so, maximum and all was spent for servers we needed, and stuff like this all 100% accounted for
>
> **B:** and i kept asking him to just meet you and go over all of these things

At the same time we had to defend ourselves against growing external pressure. On July 30, 2010, WL posted a 1.4 gigabyte encrypted file on the domain of the Afghanistan documents as well as on several Internet exchange platforms. The file is named "insurance.aes256."

I don't know what it contains. The file has been encoded using the symmetrical encryption system AES256, which makes it relatively well protected against attempts to decode it. Still, I didn't think it was a very good idea simply to post the file on the Internet. This security file was originally created to prevent anyone from destroying WL or trying to attack or take one of us out of commission in an attempt to hinder the publication of further documents. Just as other people leave their last will and testament with a lawyer, we deposited ours on the Web.

I had arduously copied the file onto USB sticks and sent them to dozens of people I trusted. Among them were Green Party politicians, journalists, and figures I knew I could rely upon.

For security reasons, I bought different types of sticks and different sorts of envelopes—brown and white, large and small. I took only a handful of them at any one time to the post office in order to prevent the entire cache from being intercepted. Some of the sticks I handed over personally. With each stick, I included a message, dated July 20:

> Entrusting you with data
> Dear friend,
>
> We are contacting you today in a matter of trust. Enclosed with this letter you can find a USB stick containing information in an encrypted archive.
>
> This information is being distributed to you and other trusted entities around the world in the

light of challenges our project might face in the
upcoming next weeks. Distribution will make sure
that no matter what happens, this information will
be disclosed to the media and consequently the
general public. It will also serve as an insurance for
the well being of our project and us.

If anything goes wrong, a second mechanism
will make sure that the keys for this material will
be distributed publicly, enabling you to decrypt
the archive and help make sure it wasn't all for
nothing.

We are entrusting you to not disclose the fact of
receiving this letter and the data to anyone. A lot might
depend on it.

With the best regards and thank you,
WikiLeaks

In the meantime, our technicians came up with a solution for
how the passwords could be made public, in case anything should
happen. The method is called the "dead-man switch." At the
time, I was unaware that there was also a plan to publish the file
on the Internet and distribute it on random download platforms.
I would have been against that, if I had known. Even if it would
take a huge amount of time and effort to decode the file, the possibility that it could happen can never be ruled out entirely.

We created the file to give ourselves some political leverage,
and I imagine we caused the people from the State Department
a few sleepless nights when they learned of its existence. An
encrypted insurance file available to everyone on the Web? On a

torrent exchange platform? That wasn't one of the standard problems described in their handbooks. It was nothing you could solve
by calling in an aircraft carrier.

I have no idea whether anyone was ultimately interested in our
security mechanism or whether it prevented the Powers That Be
from arresting us. We all, in any case, believed that it did. Later
in 2010, when Julian was sitting in protective custody after the
Swedish accusations made against him, he purportedly told his
lawyer that we would consider using the "thermonuclear device"—
that is, publicizing the key to the insurance file—if he were extradited to Sweden.

That was not what the insurance file was intended for. It was
supposed to protect WL collaborators and our documents, not to
ensure Julian avoided investigation in a democratic country, where
the investigations concern a private matter. Still, it made complete
sense to store away some especially explosive material. We should
have done it earlier, albeit perhaps with a bit less self-importance.

Our need for such a protective mechanism was confirmed, at
the latest, when our colleague Jacob Appelbaum was detained and
interrogated while trying to reenter the United States. All he had
done wrong was to speak in Julian's stead at a conference about
WikiLeaks—presumably because he thought it was important for
WL to be represented there. That was enough for US border authorities to confiscate his laptop, subject him to a search, and hold
him for several hours. Afterward, we cracked a bunch of black-
humored jokes about how now all of the contacts saved in his cell
phone were going to have problems entering the United States.

The incident was very serious for Jacob. By comparison, Julian's
tales of being pursued appear harmless. In May, when Julian's

passport was confiscated as he tried to enter Australia, the alleged scandal was passed on by news agencies around the world. Julian gave a number of interviews on Australian TV, claiming that there was no longer anywhere that he was safe. But I've seen that passport with my own eyes. It was totally mangled. The most likely story is some border-control official simply wanted to convince himself that it was indeed a form of identification and not a bit of paper fished from the trash. And the officials involved returned the passport after a few minutes.

The next thing Julian claimed was how dangerous it was for him to leave Australia. At the time, I had been scheduled to address a session of the European Parliament on the topic of Internet censorship. Julian arranged to hold the address himself, in my stead. His argument was that intelligence services would only leave him in peace if he traveled under the protection of the European Parliament. If politicians were expecting him to show up, went his reasoning, no one would dare kidnap or assassinate him. "I need political cover," he told me. I have always believed the worst we had to fear was getting beaten up by some frat boys or far-right skinheads. No one would hijack an Australian airplane to get rid of Julian Assange.

Around the same time, Julian began to increasingly involve the seventeen-year-old from Iceland in WikiLeaks. He was always warning us about the young man. He was a liar and not to be trusted, Julian said. Julian definitely wanted to prevent us from talking to him. So I was all the more astonished when the guy got his very own WL e-mail address. Very few people, fewer than twenty, had one. Julian also bought him two laptops and gave him one of the coveted Cryptophones.

In addition, Julian was becoming very careless about our security measures. E-mails to the seventeen-year-old as well as WL's spokesman Kristinn were automatically forwarded to their Gmail addresses. It was more convenient for them. I asked myself why we had to make it so easy for the Americans to snoop on our internal correspondence. And if this were really OK, why we couldn't then do without the expensive Cryptophones?

This lackadaisical approach also applied to looking after secret documents when they arrived on our server. An example was the diplomatic cables. Julian simply handed them over to one of the Icelanders, who should never have been given sensitive tasks, so that the guy could "think about how they could be worked up graphically." This guy, in turn, passed the cables on to the press—among others, to the reporter Heather Brooke from the *Guardian.* He later justified his action by saying he had asked himself how best to optimize the political effect of the material and had no choice but to "talk it over with a couple of people."

We were all acquainted with this sort of human factor, the desire to share one's secret knowledge and bolster one's own self-esteem, if need be, with the help of the press. We were supposed to be very careful about passing on information. Hadn't we already learned this lesson?

Julian, who was very paranoid about his own security, was suddenly letting the reins hang astonishingly loose. When he learned about the slipup, he sent our Icelandic journalist friends Kristinn and Ingi to confront the person concerned. But what was the use? The information was out in the world. The Icelanders made him sign a declaration saying that the documents had been taken from him illegally. It was very dangerous to have your name connected with these documents.

The seventeen-year-old also represented a growing security risk. Julian tweeted that he had been detained multiple times by the Icelandic police and told us that he had been questioned about WL. That he was shown surveillance photos and asked to identify the other individuals pictured. But those facts were never confirmed. The Icelandic police denied that anything of the sort had happened. Such tales of detention and surveillance only added to the WL mystique.

By the second half of 2010, Julian was increasingly traveling in the presence of bodyguards. What an elevation in status! At some point, I began to think that the worst of all scenarios for him would be for me to get arrested before he did. Maybe that's why he got so upset when he saw my real name on my doorbell.

The message he had sent me back in April—"If you fuck up, i will hunt you down and kill you"—hadn't done a lot to improve our relationship. But he had said this to me in a situation of stress, and often he said things to me that sounded as if they were really addressed to himself. On other occasions, he said I was a security risk because I wouldn't hold up if interrogated. I had to ask myself which planet Julian was living on. Perhaps he pictured a German policeman applying the thumbscrews while I wrote out pages and pages of a confession that were tantamount to Julian's own death sentence.

Julian once told me about regularly driving out to the woods, into the absolute middle of nowhere, to be alone for a bit and to recharge his batteries. Recalibrating, he called it. He wouldn't speak to anyone and would just pass the day without any particular goal. He said he needed to do this once every couple of months at the very least. Suddenly, two years had gone by in which he'd hardly had a day to get out into nature or even to take a stroll through a park.

A lot of people who saw him at conferences or during visits told me they thought he looked bad or seemed to be completely exhausted.

I didn't understand why we were putting ourselves under this sort of immense time pressure. Something was driving him, and I didn't know what. In 2010, we would pump out one massive release after another, as if the Grim Reaper himself were hot on our heels. Perhaps it was all the new material people were sending us.

Julian had announced in advance that we wouldn't have as much time as previously to discuss every detail. We had gotten too big, and our cause too serious, to take everything easy. He was addicted to states of emergency. Everything had to be as extreme, disruptive, and important as possible.

I saw things exactly the opposite way. Precisely because we were getting better known, and the documents more explosive, we needed to consider all the more carefully everything we did. We should have extended the self-imposed break we took in late 2009 to further develop our internal structures and we should have focused on smaller leaks until our infrastructure was on a solid footing.

I've sometimes asked myself whether Julian was afraid of anything. Whether he had any worries deep down inside and whether the new documents might not have been too hot for him. He was always saying we had to get rid of material. Once he said he was concerned that we'd get "squashed" for it. On the other hand, I never noticed any concrete signs of fear. Fear was something he simply didn't seem to feel. So there was little for him to overcome.

The result of the pressure was that we made more and more mistakes and could no longer live up to the immense responsibility we had piled upon ourselves. For Julian, this was an opportunity to spout his new favorite slogan: "Do not challenge leadership in times of crisis."

It was almost funny. Julian Assange, chief revealer of secrets and unshakable military critic on his global peace mission, had adopted the language of the powermongers he claimed to be combating. The extremely curt, soulless language of our documents, with their absurd acronyms and code words, increasingly appealed to him.

For some time, he had begun describing people as "assets," not unlike a businessman talking about "human resources" or a military man referring to his troops. Julian did not mean the word in a nice way. It showed that he saw our people as mere cannon fodder.

Later, when he tried to kick me out of WikiLeaks he said the reason was "Disloyalty, Insubordination and Destabilization in Times of Crisis." These were concepts taken from the Espionage Act of 1917, which came into force just after the United States entered World War I. They were military designations for the word "traitor."

• • •

Coded language is common in the military, and jargon is an intrinsic part of most specialized environments. Even the texts of laws that have undergone multiple revisions are often little more than gibberish. The same is true in business and finance. And the language of Scientology is even more coded than that of the military. Their handbooks are full of acronyms.

Language like this is perfectly suited to preventing outsiders from getting any insight into what is really going on. There are entire professions that justify their existence only in terms of fluency in a self-referential system. A person's actions might be completely banal in reality, but a description of them using these specialized terms would make them sound like high science. It's no wonder Julian likes jargon. Jargon is a fraudulent form of significance, in which the person who is speaking automatically seems to know what he's doing.

This is another realization I owe to working for WikiLeaks. Whether one is talking about the military, intelligence services, or strategy commissions, people are people. Some of the papers we published seemed to me, upon closer inspection, to be hair-raisingly naïve. One example was a CIA document from the Red Cell Intelligence Group, a think tank created after 9/11 to analyze problems and find creative solutions. The Red Cell paper in question concerned what kind of PR strategies America could employ to boost declining German and French support for the war in Afghanistan.

Hans-Jürgen Kleinsteuber, professor of politics in Hamburg, would describe the document as a "sophomore paper." The strategy of telling the Germans that the war was about protecting economic interests and the French that it was about the rights of women was as simpleminded as it was pernicious. It was hardly the work of especially gifted strategists. Composed in the portentous tone of the CIA, the paper may have sounded incredibly significant, but the content could have come from a junior-high-school student.

Of course, we ourselves were hardly free of this sort of self-referentiality: WikiLeaks was WL, Julian was J, I was S (for my alias last name, Schmitt), and others on the team were also referred to by individual letters. There was an internal logic to the abbreviations. The more important someone was within WL, the shorter his nickname. If you came across someone with a single initial in the WL chat room, you could be almost certain it was one of the project's official representatives.

16

Accusations in Sweden

O N August 20, 2010, Swedish prosecutors charged Julian Assange with two counts of attempted rape.

I was on vacation with my wife and our son. For two weeks we were traveling around Iceland, a country that looks like a photographic negative because the sand in lots of places is black while the frozen fjords are white. We were driving in a rental car from one village to the next, taking our time. I hadn't done anything as nice as this for years. Some days, I even managed not to think about Julian or WL for a couple of hours.

But of course, what would my life be without WL? I was repeatedly drawn to my laptop. In the car, there was a WLAN router with a UMTS mobile-phone connection, and I had a long power cord for our tent. International journalists were regularly calling me on my Icelandic cell phone.

Harvey Cashore from Canadian TV, for instance, insisted on meeting me in person. Cashore was in charge of investigative research for the Canadian Broadcasting Corporation (CBC). He was in Germany and decided to come to Iceland. We met in Isafjördur, where I had stopped on my tour with Anke and Jacob.

Cashore suggested we team up. The CBC wanted to be involved in our next publication and was prepared to put several editors at our disposal to help us process the material. I spoke with him for two hours in a fish restaurant. His efforts went unrewarded. Our other media partners refused to give the CBC a slice of the cake. The people from *Der Spiegel* were relaxed about the idea, but our English-language partners flat-out refused. Julian told me they had ratcheted up the pressure.

The German news was dominated by the catastrophe at the Love Parade on July 24 in Duisburg. Nineteen people died in a stampede at the overcrowded techno festival. Two others would succumb to their injuries a few days later.

Shortly thereafter, we began receiving a number of papers connected with the Love Parade: confidential planning documents, internal agreements, and a host of details concerning security arrangements and the permit process. It seemed as though, overnight, half of Duisburg's municipal government had gotten in touch with their inner whistle-blower.

Blogs and other media had already published some of this material, but we were definitely the first to receive such comprehensive documentation on the background of the tragedy. I felt compelled to publish the material, especially as WL had become the platform where such documents were sure to attract the proper public attention. I spent one night of my Icelandic vacation preparing everything and making sure it was fit for the website.

We had stopped in a small village named Hólmavik, which

basically consisted of a museum on witchcraft and a small, ram-
shackle guesthouse on the side of a hill. We spent a couple of
nights there. One of those nights I stayed up with Anke until five
in the morning, working on the Duisburg material in the small
common area that served as the breakfast room. There was a pile
of beer cans next to me from previous guests, and I was wearing dark-blue merino-wool long johns and thick socks against
the cold. The only thing that helped combat the painfully slow
Internet connection was patience. I had to go through some forty
documents and restart the entire chain of production, which was
scheduled for revision but which had been neglected because the
completion of our most recent publication had consumed such
immense resources. One task was to read through all the documents and sort out which were different versions of the same
thing. I also had to write summaries and create publishable documents with cover letters. Since our "strike" we had only published
bigger leaks on specially dedicated websites—this was to be our
first normal publication since resuming operations.

The Love Parade documents went online on August 20.
Although it had originally been something of an ironclad principle, by this point we were no longer publishing material in the
order in which it arrived. We concentrated on the really big stuff.
Julian had issued orders to that effect and had refused to yield
despite heated discussions about whether this was right, and
despite the fact that, in my eyes, a lot of important material was
being ignored.

For example, we possessed the e-mail correspondence over the
past four years of the far-right German political party NPD. I had
given a journalist a selection of the material so that he could get

a first impression, and *Der Spiegel,* which was also apparently in possession of at least some of the documents, had already written an article. The original version of the piece had cited some of the e-mails, and the party had succeeded in getting a temporary injunction against the magazine. The injunction was later rescinded, but publishing the material would have been good for us. It would have underscored our advantages vis-à-vis traditional media. Injunctions were of no use against WL since there was no official recipient.

When we returned to Reykjavík the following Friday, I logged on to the chat room and discovered what seemed to be a problem. One of the techies, who had also gone on vacation, had disappeared. He'd been gone for nine days even though he had originally said he would only be away for three. We regularly checked to see that our people arrived safely at appointments and that no one had been detained at borders or had gone missing. We were worried.

During our tour of Iceland, we had slept in different beds almost every night, and before our son went to sleep, my wife would tell him that whatever he dreamed of would come true. I don't know whether this made much of an impression on Jacob, but it sure did on me. That night I dreamed that our colleague had returned home safe and sound from an adventure, and the next morning I awoke convinced that everything would be all right.

And indeed, when I logged on to the chat room, our friend was back. But the good news was followed by a massive blow.

Twenty minutes later, when I entered "WikiLeaks" into Google News, I learned that a warrant for Julian's arrest had been issued in Sweden. He was alleged to have raped two women.

Normally, Swedish law protects people who are the subject of investigations. To avoid damaging their reputations, the media aren't even allowed to publish the ages, let alone the names, of suspects. But in this case, the Swedish tabloid *Expressen,* which, like the publishers of some editions of this book, is part of Sweden's Bonnier Group, had broken all the rules. The paper had written a story based on the prosecutor's initial investigations and published it with all the names and details. Julian was caught completely unaware. He hadn't even been formally summoned by the police. The first he'd heard about the accusations was from *Expressen.* You wouldn't wish something like that on your worst enemy.

What was strange was that suddenly, for the first time in months, I felt as though Julian was listening to me again. At least when the news first broke. He needed my advice. He needed to hear from everyone that they were on his side. We later advised him to step back from the spotlight for a while. At the same time, we confirmed that we were completely behind him and saw no reason to doubt his version of events.

I was back in Reykjavík with Anke and Jacob to take in the city's annual cultural festival after enjoying the isolation of the Icelandic countryside. It was Saturday, and the streets were full of people. Stands had been set up everywhere; there was food, drink, and music; and the Reykjavík Marathon was taking place on some of the city's major avenues. In front of the old jailhouse, Birgitta was reading some of her poetry and collecting signatures supporting an environmental campaigner. I left Anke and Jacob

behind at a group of stands and fought my way through the Hall-
grímskirkja, a Protestant church that vaguely resembles a launch-
ready Ariane space rocket. I had agreed to meet Ingi and Kristinn
there to discuss our current problem.

The two Icelanders were waiting for me next to the statue of
Leif Ericsson. Kristinn had a habit of looking through people,
as though he had seen something frightening in his past and
decided to avoid direct eye contact. Ingi stood a bit to the rear,
his hands folded in front of his chest. He was wearing olive-green
or khaki-colored pants and a vest and was carrying a well-worn
messenger bag.

We walked for a while and went into the Einar Jónsson Museum. We weren't interested in the sculptures there, but we kept
walking as we talked, tracing a path of curves and loops: up a
flight of stairs and down again on the other side, around a set of
revolving doors to the right, in a figure eight through the room
on the left and then back up the stairs to the second floor. A back
door led us out into the sculpture garden. If anyone had been tail-
ing us, we would have tired him out, if not shaken him off.

We paused for a moment between the bronze figures. Kristinn
was chain-smoking and overarticulated his words. He kept inter-
rupting me. He had spent considerable time with Julian in Great
Britain and could count himself among Julian's most intimate
associates.

"What do we do now?" I asked.

Kristinn looked right through me. Ingi observed us, saying
nothing. It was clear to me that our crisis-management strategy
was somewhere between nonexistent and miserable, and that
we all desperately needed to get together as a group and have a

fundamental rethink about roles, tasks, and structures. There was no way we could solve our problems in the chat room. I had been pleading for such a core meeting for quite some time. Birgitta joined the three of us a bit later. She, too, seemed at a loss about how to handle our current situation.

Then Kristinn's cell phone rang. He listened for a while, then answered gleefully and informed us that the warrant had been temporarily suspended. What a day!

Nonetheless, I still thought Julian should rethink his behavior toward his female acquaintances.

There are indeed a few things to be said on the topic of Julian and women. Julian liked women, that's crystal clear. But there was no one woman with whom he was preoccupied—he liked the idea of women in general. Whenever we attended conferences, he would often scope out the scene. He wasn't particularly interested in legs, breasts, or asses like the stereotypical man. Julian's attraction to women wasn't as predictable as it was portrayed in the media. Julian had an eye for details—wrists, shoulders, or necks, for example. He never said anything like "Great tits." He would say things along the lines of "That woman has amazing cheekbones—she looks very aristocratic." Once we noticed an extremely graceful woman searching through her handbag as she passed, and Julian said, "It must feel nice to be touched by those hands." That was as far as he went. He never said anything obscene to me about women.

I must admit that his fascination with women was contagious, even though I was already spoken for. I remember at the Global

Voices Summit in Budapest, we attended a party after our lecture. It took place on the roof of a former supermarket, and we ended up drinking a lot of absinthe. Julian and I normally weren't big drinkers, but we were in a pretty jolly mood as we made our way from the party back to our apartment.

The apartment had a small gas leak, probably from a faulty pipe, and smelled terrible. We took turns sleeping in the bunk bed and on the sofa. We joked about the smell of gas: "If you hear me taking my last gasp in my sleep, get to the window." Or "Do you have any final words for your parents when I break the sad news?" But the apartment was cheap and centrally located. Life was actually pretty good in Budapest.

On our way back home from our absinthe evening, we both saw what amounted to an apparition. A woman in hot pants and a tight top whizzed past us on Rollerblades. We continued talking about the conference, other people we knew, and our future plans, but every once in a while, one of us would sigh and say, "What a woman!" Or "Boy, was she the business!" Later, we repeatedly came back to the woman on Rollerblades. She became something of a symbol for our ideal woman.

I never slept around during my time with WL, but I was still plagued by a bad conscience. I noticed that all the travel had put distance between me and my girlfriend in Wiesbaden.

Julian's main criterion for a woman was simple. She had to be young. Preferably younger than twenty-two. And it went without saying that she couldn't question him. "She has to be aware of her role as a woman," he used to say. She was also allowed to be intelligent—Julian liked that.

I never noticed him going for any one particular type. It didn't matter whether a woman was thin or fat, big or small, blond or brunette. It was fine if she was good-looking, but that wasn't the be-all and end-all. At least, that's the way he seemed to me when we attended conferences together.

For a time I thought that something might be beginning to develop between him and Birgitta. Birgitta was anything but submissive. She was a straight-ahead sort of woman who spoke her mind. She's unquestionably attractive, but she's a long way from being twenty-two. At some point, Julian said to me that she was his dream woman. But maybe he just said that because he often felt the need to say something drastically significant. My sense was that he would never be able to accept a woman who was truly his equal.

We often discussed the theory of evolution. If he did have faith in anything, it was the theory of evolution. Julian thought that the stronger members of the species not only prevailed, but produced heirs who were better able to survive. Naturally, in his view, his genes particularly deserved to be reproduced.

Often I sat in larger groups and listened to Julian boast about how many children he had fathered in various parts of the world. He seemed to enjoy the idea of lots and lots of little Julians, one on every continent. Whether he took care of any of these alleged children, or whether they existed at all, was another question.

But Julian could also be very forthcoming with women. When he met a woman for the first time, he was polite and charming. He never paid her too much attention, though, and that seemed to keep her coming back for more. His lack of interest was attractive.

• • •

In any case, Julian's alleged refusal to wear condoms was a basis of the accusations against him in Sweden. Anna A., one of the women who prompted the investigations, is a member of that country's Association of Christian Social Democrats. She had invited Julian to a seminar in Stockholm on the role of the media in conflict situations. What really happened between them is known only to the women in question and Julian.

The main thing for me was that the accusations existed, and Julian's position at WL required us to take an official stance toward them. An international warrant for the arrest of a leader of an organization damages the reputation of the project he represents. What one does about it is another issue. The only thing I and others asked him to do was step back from the spotlight a bit. He, on the other hand, began to blame the whole thing on a smear campaign by the Pentagon. He said he had been warned, not long before the accusations, that dirty tricks would be used against him, and that he should be careful not to fall into a sex trap. He refused to tell us which of his contacts had warned him, but he assured us his sources were reliable.

We discussed the issue in the chat room:

> **J:** they will go away be the end of the week
>
> **D:** no, they wont
>
> **D:** what will happen given that nothing happens, is that more people will come out of the closet
>
> **D:** because people do not like the way this is being dealt with
>
> **D:** its pretty dead simple
>
> **D:** they want to see this has a consequence

D: and given the statements you made, plus the fact that we are even trying to push this while setup-angle, this is not what is expected

D: whole*

D: this is all not what will make people that feel hurt or whatever go away, in contrary so

D: the reaction to it triggers people to come out of the closet

J: that's the line you're trying to push around?

D: what line?

J: if so, i will destroy you.

D: lol

D: wtf [what the fuck] j

D: seriously

D: whats that bullshit?

D: are you out of your fuckin mind?

D: i am not taking this bs much longer j

D: seriously

D: you are shooting a messenger here, and this is not acceptible

D: the one that faces serious problems is you

D: and by that the project might be harmed

D: and thats my concern

D: my interest in helping you does not really thrive the way you are dealing with this

D: cant even believe this

D: have you ever, just once, in all this hybris you seem trapped in considered that not everything is someone elses fault?

D: good luck man, i am tired of doing damage control for you there

D: so take a pick

J: Go away and think about your actions and statements. I know of many you do not think I do. I will not tolerate disloyalty in crisis.

D: i think you misunderstand the situation here j

D: quite frankly

D: but as i said, i will not cover for you anymore or do any further damage control

D: good luck with your attitude

D: i for myself have nothing i need to be ashamed for

J: So be it

How was I supposed to make it clear that I was only concerned about the project? In his eyes, we had all fallen for the smear campaign and were now betraying him.

He had told me about the two women. He denied having slept with them without a condom. When asked about the details of the accusations, he remained vague. I have no desire to pass judgment on the women, or on Julian's conduct. Above all, what apparently sealed his fate in this case was the fact that a sexist guy like him had come together with a pair of emancipated women in a country with stricter judicial standards concerning sexual conduct than most other nations. His pop status, among other things, had gotten him into a situation that was beyond his control.

The question arose of who should pay Julian's legal costs. It wasn't right for him to simply use money from funds donated to WikiLeaks. The accusations were a private matter. I wouldn't have objected if he had submitted a bill for his past year's work to the foundation or whomever. That would have given him enough money for his attorney, and everything would have been above-board. I tried on a number of occasions in the chat room to suggest this as an option. But Julian refused to consider it.

17

My Suspension

THE day after the news broke of the first arrest warrant against Julian in Sweden, I flew back to Berlin and barricaded myself in our apartment. For a time, all I did was just sit in our living room, at the large table with the view of the construction site, with my laptop open, staring at the chat and occasionally contributing to it. I hardly ever went to the club in Berlin, although it had been my habit to do work there most days. It was obvious that something was getting me down, and I didn't want anyone to ask me what it was.

There was nothing Anke could do. No doubt she would have loved to have said "Let it go. It's destroying you." But she knew how much of my heart I had invested in WL and that I probably wouldn't take kindly to any such suggestion—in part because I would have known myself that she was right.

I also realized, though, that step-by-step I was mentally divorcing myself from WikiLeaks. Admittedly, the personal conflicts between Julian and me were a major catalyst, perhaps even the most important reason behind the rupture. But there were also a lot of substantive points that had concerned me for some time and that would become even more acute in the days to come. I had long had a problem with deceiving the public about our internal structure, concealing the fact that WL had initially consisted of two individuals and a single server. I was also very worried about our inadequate backup system. Ultimately I was the one who was responsible if it didn't function correctly. More than once in the past two years, I had woken up in the middle of the night, panicked by the thought that something had gone wrong. I would leap out of bed with more adrenaline than blood in my veins and make additional backup copies.

Another issue was our "authenticity checks"—a deceit I had forced myself to practice in hundreds of interviews. Until late 2009, no one except Julian and I checked the vast majority of documents that had been submitted. Strictly speaking, we weren't lying when we said we had a pool of around eight hundred volunteer experts at our disposal. But we neglected to mention that we had no mechanism in place for integrating them into our workflow. None of them were able to access the material we received. Instead, Julian and I usually checked whether documents had been manipulated technologically and did a few Google searches to see whether they struck us as genuine. We could only hope that things would turn out all right. Apparently we developed a pretty good sense for what was authentic and what wasn't; at least as far as I know, we didn't make any major mistakes. But we could have.

I could suppress these qualms as long as I was able to tell myself that we were just starting out, that we were working on a better system. But after almost three years, I no longer believed this myself. In the preceding months, we had had the opportunity to commit ourselves to the improvements we had always said we

wanted to make. There was money and there were a couple of reliable assistants at our disposal. But we didn't sufficiently tackle the
problem. We were acting irresponsibly, playing a risky game with
our sources' trust and our supporters' donations.

In the old days, Julian was the only one with whom I could
discuss such problems. After all, he was as aware as anyone of our
internal shortcomings. But I was reticent to raise any concerns. I
didn't want to start any more conflicts. So I had taken to exchanging views with the architect and Birgitta, as well as with Herbert
Snorrason and Harald Schumann at the *Tagesspiegel* newspaper.
The chat room in which we discussed these issues, and became
increasingly worried, had a very revealing name: Mission First.

It had been clear for quite some time that WL was headed in
the wrong direction and that we were going to have to change
course. The architect had already started with the technical
restructuring. But the more we discussed the problems, the more
obvious it became that far more extensive restructuring was
needed. In Iceland, Schumann had repeatedly asked who among
us was making the decisions. He was very persistent, posing this
question day in and day out at the Ministry of Ideas, never satisfied with our answers. We became evasive. We tried to avoid him
or change the subject. That was precisely our problem.

We had tried to come up with principles to resolve all the
critical questions. For example, to ensure our neutrality we had
pledged to simply publish everything we received in the order in
which it was submitted. But by the end of 2009 at the latest, we
could no longer adhere to this ideal. We were swamped by submissions. Choices had to be made.

We had also conceived of ourselves as a neutral submission

platform, pure technology, and not a political agitator with a Twitter account. But we had chosen specific media partners to work with and in so doing had placed ourselves in a position of dependency. At first, cooperating with newspapers and magazines had just been a trial balloon, but it soon became standard operating procedure. We enjoyed the limelight the media gave us and told ourselves that our new way of doing things made the content of our material much more easily accessible.

The great advantage in not making qualitative distinctions between individual documents and publications was that, if things went wrong, no one was personally responsible. Instead, we wanted to rely on principles and automatic mechanisms. But that was wishful thinking. We had no choice but to make decisions, and we did so without defining any rules for the process. Schumann had hit the nail right on the head with his question: Who had the final say?

Ultimately, of course, it was Julian who made the decisions. The rest of us were too indecisive and skittish or simply lacked the resolve to set any limits for him. Julian thus became the autocratic head of WL, accountable to no one and tolerating no challenges to his authority. This had emerged as a problem when Bradley Manning was arrested, and clearly it was going to be a problem in the weeks to come. The investigations in Sweden would prove to be the wedge that finally broke up our team.

Within twenty-four hours of the affair becoming public, the Swedish prosecutor had withdrawn the arrest warrant against Julian and reduced the charges from rape to sexual harassment. But in November 2010, the attorney for the two women in question succeeded in getting the rape accusation reinstated.

In the wake of our crisis meeting in the sculpture garden, Kristinn reported back to Julian that I had tried to manipulate Birgitta. Or at least Julian later claimed Kristinn had said that. Debates about who had said what to whom were to become one of our main activities in the days and weeks that followed.

We had started making transcripts of our chats and swapping them among ourselves. It was our way of combating Julian's "symmetrical" understanding of the truth. We only wanted there to be something approaching genuine documents, evidence of what had been discussed. No one would have had any objections, either, to Kristinn and Ingi participating in our discussions, although I did not consider them members of the core team. If there's one thing I learned from my time at WL it's that important questions should always be discussed by the group, and that no one should be excluded from the discussion.

A copy of the chat in which Julian announced my suspension was published in *Wired* magazine. To this day, I don't know who passed it on, but I think there are good reasons for letting other people have a look at the transcript. It does not deal with private issues, but with the culture of communication within WikiLeaks, a project whose battle cry was, more than any other organization, transparency. The chat transcripts reveal the state the project was in at the time, and the tone of voice and arguments that were used. They provide the sorts of insights I can neither explain nor make a case for with subjective descriptions. I can claim a hundred times over that Julian became a dictator. Instead, everyone should make up his or her own mind by reading the chats.

Only a few days had passed since the charges in Sweden had been issued, when, on a Wednesday evening, the infighting resumed on the daily WL staff chat. Julian emphasized that he had no time to fill us in on the logic behind his decisions because he had "high level discussions with around 20 people a day now." I have no idea who he meant. Perhaps Julian's so-called assistants were traveling around with him, attending meetings, or accompanying him to interview shoots. I don't know. At the time, Julian was still in Sweden. As far as I know, he had contact there with some people from the Pirate Party and some journalists at the Swedish daily *Aftonbladet,* for which he was supposed to begin writing a column. There's no doubt that it would have been important to get more reliable people involved in WL and take the pressure off the core team.

At the time, we were fighting a lot about an article in the *Wall Street Journal.* The journalists had asked me and Julian independently about our finances. I had told them how transparently and regularly our donations were recorded in Germany. Julian had told them the exact opposite, saying that WL accounts were skillfully and explicitly managed to prevent them from being attacked by anyone on the outside. In the article, he portrayed our nontransparent bookkeeping as a clever method for preventing our enemies from shutting off our cash flow.

That, of course, only attracted a host of other curious journalists who wanted to know why we were concealing our finances. Above all, it meant that the Wau Holland Foundation had a lot of explaining to do. Julian would later claim he had been misquoted.

In the chat room, we again asked him to step back and to stop talking to the press and sending out tweets describing the charges as a Pentagon smear campaign. When our questions got too critical, though, Julian would simply log himself out.

I think that he was taken aback that we had stood up to him so forcefully and that, in particular, the architect refused to budge an inch from his critical position. I thought it was important to hear what our other main techie had to say on this issue. But he preferred to stay out of the fight.

The two techies and I were almost at our wits' end. I had spent three hours in the chat room, and we were further away from a solution than ever. The debate had been going on for weeks. We wanted to make Julian talk to us. In the end we resorted to a fairly draconian measure, a shot in the dark. Perhaps it wasn't the best way to tackle the problem. But we wanted to make clear to him that WikiLeaks was heading toward a mutiny. So we used the one small advantage we possessed—as technicians—and just let a few systems go down. Nothing major, nothing nasty. Just a symbolic act of protest.

On August 25, 2010, the architect and technician switched the system onto maintenance mode. The submission system, the e-mail system, and the chat room remained online. Only the wiki was down. We tweeted to say there was temporary maintenance work going on. We also changed the password for accessing the Twitter and e-mail accounts. We were trying to shake Julian up.

In response, Julian shut down the whole system. We caved in almost immediately, restored the wiki, and gave him the passwords.

The next day, an article appeared in *Newsweek* about infighting at WikiLeaks. I hadn't heard anything about it until Julian mentioned it to me via the chat. Julian assumed that I was the source of the news. He was wrong. I had never talked to *Newsweek*. I didn't even know the reporter. Originally, I had wanted to ask about our arrangements for the upcoming Iraq leak. But the chat took a different turn.

D: what are the agreements re iraq? i need to understand what the plan is there, and what the constraints are

J: "A person in close contact with other WikiLeaks activists around Europe, who asked for anonymity when discussing a sensitive topic, says that many of them were privately concerned that Assange has continued to spread allegations of dirty tricks and hint at conspiracies against him without justification. Insiders say that some people affiliated with the website are already brainstorming whether there might be some way to persuade their front man to step aside, or failing that, even to oust him."

D: what does that have to do with me?

D: and where is this from?

J: Why do you think it has something to do with you?

D: probably because you alleg this was me

D: but other than that just about nothing

D: as discussed yesterday, this is an ongoing discussion that lots of people have voiced concern about

D: you should face this, rather than trying to shoot at the only person that even cares to be honest about it towards you

J: No, three people have "relayed" your messages already.

D: what messages?

D: and what three people?

D: this issue was discussed

D: A [Architect] and i talked about it, Hans* talked about it, B talked it, Peter* talked about it ow many people at the club?

D: i dont have to answer to you on this j

D: this debate is fuckin all over the place, and no one understands why you go into denial [...]

J: How many people at the club?

J: In what venue?

D: in private chats

D: but i will not answer anymore of these questions

D: face the fact that you have not much trust on the inside anymore

D: and that just denying it or putting it away as a campaign against you will not change that it is solely a consequence of your actions

D: and not mine

J: How many people are represented by these private chats? And what are there positions in the CCC?

D: go figure

D: i dont even wanna think about how many people that used to respect you told me that they feel disappointed by your reactions

D: i tried to tell you all this, but in all your hybris you dont even care

D: so i dont care anymore either

D: other than that, i had questions first, and i need answers

D: like what agreements we have made

D: i need to understand this so we can continue working

D: you keep stalling other peoples work

J: How many people are represented by these private chats? And what are there positions in the CCC?

D: start answering my questions j

J: This is not a quid-pro-quo.

J: Are you refusing to answer?

D: i have already told you again that i dont see why

i should answer to you anymore just because you
want answers, but on the same hand refuse to answer
anything i am asking

D: i am not a dog you can contain the way you want to j

J: i am investigation a serious security breach. Are
you refusing to answer?

D: i am investigating a serious breach in trust. are you
refusing to answer?

J: No you are not. I initiated this conversation. Answer
the question please.

D: i initiated it

D: if you look above

D: twice already

D: i want to know what the agreements are in respect to
iraq

J: That is a procedural issue. Don't play games with me.

D: stop shooting at messengers

J: I've had it.

D: likewise, and that doesnt go just for me

J: If you do not answer the question, you will be removed.

D: you are not anyones king or god

D: and you're not even fulfilling your role as a leader
right now

D: a leader communicates and cultivates trust in himself

D: you are doing the exact opposite

D: you behave like some kind of emporer or slave trader

J: You are suspended for one month, effective immediately.

D: haha

D: right

D: because of what?

D: and who even says that?

D: you? another adhoc decision?

J: If you wish to appeal, you will be heard on Tuesday.

D: BAHAHAHA

D: maybe everyone was right, and you really have gone
mental j

D: you should get some help

J: You will be heard by a panel of peers.

J: You are suspend for disloyalty, insubordination and
destabalization in a time of crisis.

A few hours after my suspension, on the evening of August 26, Julian called a meeting. The architect, the technician, and I were barred from participating. The nanny, Birgitta, and Kristinn were among those who did take part. A friend of mine had logged in under the name of Resa*, as well as several other people whom Julian had mobilized. Herbert Snorrason, my anarchist friend from Iceland, also took part and sent me the transcript of the chat afterward. The architect and I later added our comments and forwarded the transcript to all those concerned.

The topic of the meeting was our act of mutiny and my suspension. "Daniel is problematic, and, frankly, delusional," Julian wrote, "an illmotivated, but he can be kept in a box if he has other people telling him what is wrong and right and what he can do and can not do. when he is left in his germanic bubble he floats."

Julian was clearly trying to win over the others, but they weren't easily convinced. They kept asking questions and criticizing

Julian for deciding things on his own rather than discussing them with the team. For me, the eighty-nine-page transcript had all the suspense of a good detective story. It made clear, to me and probably also to Julian, that while the others would not rebel openly, he also didn't have a majority of them on his side.

Julian particularly hoped to keep the architect on the team; he needed him more than anyone else. The architect was central to our infrastructure. He was the one who had revised the submission system in late 2009. Previously it had been a simple upload formula embedded in the website. He had separated the various platforms of the server, the wiki, and the e-mail system so that hackers would not be able to penetrate the entire system. There are few people in the entire world who would have been able to do this.

That made me understand all the less why Julian failed to sufficiently appreciate the architect's work. And he drove the architect away, once and for all, with the chat meeting by portraying him as an unwitting stooge who had fallen under my pernicious influence.

Julian must have suspected at this stage that the planned hearing could very easily have gone against him. Even if he had hand-picked the "panel of peers," how could he have been sure that the panel wouldn't have opposed my suspension and perhaps challenged his supreme authority at WikiLeaks?

In hindsight, suspending me had the advantage of allowing Julian to claim that I was just a frustrated member of staff trying to get revenge by criticizing the project. I was indeed frustrated. By this point emotions had boiled over. But the origin of my criticism was not frustration at my suspension, and in the meantime, the others were also reaching the conclusion that something at WL was going drastically wrong.

By suspending me, Julian ensured that I was shut out of various systems and restricted in my ability to communicate. In the past I had access to everything, theoretically, including Julian's own e-mails. I never read them, though.

Like many of us, I used my e-mail account to save appointments and contacts, so I no longer had access to my own commitments in the following weeks. I had agreed to give at least four or five lectures at various upcoming conferences. For instance, Thomas Leif, the chairman of the Hambach Castle Democracy Forum, had invited me to attend an event called "My Data Belongs to You." I couldn't even get in touch with him to cancel. My chair on the stage remained empty.

I tried later to apologize to all of the people I inadvertently let down. Sometimes I still worry that there is someone who is really angry with me because I left him sitting alone on a podium somewhere.

18

Quitting WikiLeaks

I WASN'T the only one Julian had barred from the e-mail server. He'd excluded everyone else, too. He alone had access. I was the one who laid the necessary groundwork for many of the tasks carried out by the technicians. That was bad enough. But combined with the fact that he had prevented everyone else from accessing the e-mail server, it meant no one could do their work. The Iraq publications needed to be processed. The domain administration also ran from the e-mail server, and we desperately needed to set up subdomains for the Iraq documents.

We had agreed on a date of the publication with our media partners, *Der Spiegel,* the *Guardian,* and the *New York Times.* That date now had to be put back by a month—to October 23, 2010. Julian blamed it all on me.

We were in a strange state of limbo. On the one hand, my "trial" still hadn't taken place and I was officially "suspended." On the other, we were still in contact via chat. Julian sent me endless complaints. He told me he was wasting all his time repairing damage that I had caused. It was a bit like having an ex-girlfriend spending an hour a day leaving messages on my answering machine, telling me that she didn't ever want to have anything to do with me again. Of course, I wasn't any more reasonable and kept sniping back at him.

On the condition that no one reveal the password to me, under any circumstances, he offered to reinstate the techies' access to the system. They refused. Neither of them agreed with my suspension. The architect clearly took my side. The young technician kept out of the fray. He was suffering because things weren't moving forward. He just wanted us to carry on as before.

Julian had said that he wanted to put together a "panel of peers." We spent the next few days waiting for him to get in touch and name the tribunal. It was a mystery who these "peers" would be—Julian would only say that he needed the panel "so that the process was seen to be transparent and others would have confidence."

Birgitta had talked to a journalist from the *Daily Beast,* and the resulting article sparked the next controversy. She had said, among other things, that Julian had a "chauvinistic relationship" to women. And that she had advised him to step aside for a while. Julian freaked out. He felt betrayed.

Birgitta had underestimated the trouble the article would unleash. Later she sent a message via Twitter to try to calm the speculation sparked by her statement: "I did NOT suggest Assange should resign, I think he should not be a spokesman right now. He still has my support for all his other work." But she never apologized for talking to the press. She always spoke her mind and stood by it.

Julian was convinced that I had manipulated Birgitta to say what she did in the *Daily Beast* article. He also believed that I was the source of the information about the internal squabbles at

WikiLeaks. I hadn't talked to any journalists, and I don't know to this day where the journalist in question got his information. Perhaps he simply invented the quote he used about internal differences. With different opinions being aired in the press, it wasn't too difficult to conclude that we were split internally. Birgitta had said that she thought it would be best if Julian stepped aside for a while, while he maintained that the women in Sweden had been working for the Pentagon and that he was the victim of a smear campaign. The rape allegations, he wrote, meant that he had just been through "the worst week in my life in the past 10 years." As a result, he claimed, he had been unable to organize my hearing in front of the "panel of peers."

He also accused us in general of not being sufficiently worried about him. Three days later, on September 7, he sent us a whole list of things that, in his opinion, we had failed to consider adequately:

> Awareness comes from motivation. Ensured my legal
> support? Housing? Money supply? Intelligence about
> the case? Details about why it is happening? My support
> network in Sweden? Political approaches to stop the
> smear? Articles? Tipoffs? Safehouses? False papers?
> Diplomatic invites so I won't be shipped off to the
> US? Rally supports? Raise money for my case? Done
> any of that? Why not? I do all of that when one of us
> goes down.

For my part, I had at least helped him get two good lawyers in Sweden. I did that the very day I heard about the charges, while I was still on vacation.

· · ·

Suddenly the mail server crashed, and Julian was locked out too. I don't know if he was responsible. Maybe the thing just gave up the ghost. The piece of junk was old enough. It was the only server we hadn't updated.

In any case, a discussion commenced about whether I should go and repair it, something I had done on quite a few occasions in the past. The trip, I thought, would give me an opportunity to access my e-mails so at least I would know whom to apologize to for not showing up.

On September 10 or 11, I got on a train. It was a very hot late-summer day. The train wasn't particularly full, and luckily, the few people in my open-seating compartment were all preoccupied with their own affairs. I spent the whole time typing in the chat window of my computer and tapping on the floor with my feet. I continued the discussion in the chat room, unsure of whether I was doing the right thing. Should I in fact access the server without Julian's knowledge? It was a matter of conscience: should we mutiny?

The server was located in a nondescript town in the Ruhr region of western Germany. It was a long journey, and I had plenty of time to think things over. After three hours I decided to turn around. I can't remember the name of the station, but as we pulled in I grabbed my backpack, pressed a button to open the train door, and jumped out onto the platform. It was like when you spot a police car in your rearview mirror and suddenly get the irrational feeling that you've done something wrong. That was the way I felt. I went back to Berlin.

After my suspension, the architect had put away his keyboard and refused to write a single line for WL—either in the form of programming code or in conversation with Julian. It was a kind of solidarity strike. The architect is a pragmatic person who usually doesn't let himself get worked up about anything. But he does get angry when someone wastes his time. One time, after Julian had failed to respond to the architect's repeated queries about why he was no longer getting any feedback, the architect had warned him, "If things continue like this, I'm out of here." When the situation continued to escalate, he made good on his threat.

Julian got in touch with me and asked why the architect had gone AWOL. What was I supposed to say?

I had discussed with a few of the others whether it would make sense for us to take over the project. We spent ages considering whether we should turn the whole hierarchy on its head, seize the rudder, and suspend Julian. We were the majority. Theoretically, we all had the same rights. A lot of people advised us: "Why don't you take over technical control and make sure that he can't create any more trouble?" But we didn't want to do anything that major against Julian's will.

On September 14, I set off for the computer center again. I switched off my cell phone and computer for the duration of the journey and did my best to read a book. I wanted to force myself to remain firm.

I had tried to contact the person who had registered the server for us but hadn't managed to get in touch with him. He didn't know a lot about what had been going on recently, but he had reacted very skeptically when I had told him about my first trip. To him, it sounded as if we were doing something behind Julian's back. It didn't matter how many times I told him that I just wanted to get the server back up to speed again so we could continue our work.

I stared out the train window, letting the trees, the houses, and the landscape rush past. This time I wasn't going to turn around. I just blanked out the negative thoughts and hoped that everything would be OK.

Computer centers are often located in inconspicuous office buildings, unidentifiable from the outside. I walked through a few soulless gray corridors, took an elevator to the second floor, said hello to whomever was there, and headed for our server. No one stopped me. A computer center of that kind houses servers for many disparate companies. Security is tight. But because I had repaired things there on several occasions, people knew me and didn't ask questions.

I waited impatiently for the server to boot up. My laptop was next to me. I was online, of course, and in touch with the others. I didn't feel very comfortable. It was much too hot in the data center, and I was sweating. The air-conditioning unit was humming loudly, but pumping out far too little cool air. It was no wonder our ancient machine broke down.

One of the guys from the center came into the room. I said hello and he nodded back. He checked a setting and disappeared again.

When I looked up again about fifteen minutes later, he was suddenly standing in front of me. I jumped. I hadn't even heard him coming into the room. He looked as if he was about to say something. I had already prepared my explanation. But maybe he just wanted to look me straight in the eye to make sure that he really recognized me. He nodded again and left the room.

The computer finally rebooted. I stared at my screen. Someone new had popped up in the chat room, and I knew immediately who it was. The contact who had rented the server for us.

"What are you doing?" he asked without saying hello.

"I'm here at the server," I wrote back.

"I know. The center informed me. What on earth are you up to?"

"Listen, I'm just carrying out repairs. I'm not doing anything that anyone should have a problem with."

"I've been in contact with Julian. He freaked out."

"He has no reason to."

"He says he's going to call the police."

"That's silly, listen . . ."

"I'd like you to keep your hands off it, Daniel, OK? Get out of there before anything happens. Julian is saying that he'll have you arrested."

"Wait . . ."

But there was no point discussing things. I wasn't sure whether Julian would really call the police. Even if the police took away our server, it was encrypted, and they wouldn't be able to do anything with it. But the server would have been gone. And a visit from the police might have created difficulties for our contact.

I was well acquainted with Julian's exaggerated threats. But out of respect for the person who had taken a risk on our behalf and registered the server in his name, I decided to back off.

I had only repaired the server. I hadn't manipulated it or even copied my own e-mails. Julian and the others could access their e-mails again.

The reaction was devastating. Julian went on a rampage. He refused to type in the code to put the server back in service and wrote to me: "Try that again and I'll have you locked up." He said that the server would have to be sent to "forensics" because it had been manipulated, either by me or by the secret service. I didn't have a clue what he was talking about. Did he mean that the server would have to be taken to the police, or to a special laboratory where he would have it examined? One way or another, it would have been complete nonsense.

Julian popped up in the chat room, even though there was a meeting planned there for the following day. "The talk is now because the crime was today," he wrote. Birgitta and Herbert were logged on, and suddenly the architect appeared as well. The discussion had arisen spontaneously. It was September 14. I was really glad that we were finally talking to one another. I didn't suspect that this conversation would be our last.

I didn't know how often I had sat in the past few days, staring at the screen for hours, my eyes not really focused, just waiting for a small button to appear and indicate that Julian was present. I barely left our apartment—only when it was absolutely necessary. And no matter what I did, whether I popped out for some milk or went to the dentist, I always hoped that I would see something on the screen the next time that I looked at it. A message from Julian to me.

I carried my laptop with me wherever I went: into the kitchen, the living room, even to the bathtub. When I went to bed, it was there at my side. It wasn't as if I didn't have better things to do, but I couldn't help myself. At some stage, I started seeing green letters regardless of what I was looking at. The world had turned into one big chat window. And because I had been waiting so long for a message, my imagination began to dream them up out of the blue.

238

Inside WikiLeaks

"Hey Daniel, i have to talk to you."

"I've been thinking. Maybe I misunderstood things. Let's talk about the future of WL."

"Maybe we should meet and clear up the misunderstandings. Hey, you know we really had a great time together with those artsy-fartsies in Linz, or the bears, do you remember?!"

I was an incorrigible dreamer. A starry-eyed idealist. It was time to wake up and smell the coffee. What Julian actually wrote was "If you threaten this organization again, you will be attended to."

And: "Daniel has a disease, it's some kind of borderline paranoid schizophrenia." And: "You are a criminal."

Julian was once again acting as if he alone had all the say at WL. Julian wrote that he had composed 99 percent of the summaries and editorials and all the tweets, and that the entire philosophy of the project was his doing. "So what you are saying Julian," Birgitta responded, "is that YOU are wl and everyone else just your servants whom you allocate trust to."

The architect was also having none of this and made it clear that it was best for everyone if we went our separate ways. He was prepared to return control over the system, but he would return it in the state in which he had found it a year before.

Julian responded, "Our duties are bigger than this idiocy," adding that the architect was only "a shadow of the man you were."

He also demanded an apology from Birgitta for going behind his back and speaking to the journalist from the *Daily Beast*. "Listen to me very carefully. It was backstabbing and it was disgraceful and you should apologise. Do you apologise?"

Instead, Birgitta reiterated her criticism of Julian's response to the Swedish charges. She wrote, "You have mixed wl with this in a very bad way."

Julian replied, "No. WL has sabotaged my private life."

Julian then suggested that he and the architect withdraw to a parallel chat room for a private talk. That was the last straw.

The architect wrote: "Well you had 5 minutes time . . . you blew it. have fun. dont waste my time (how many times do i have to tell you that?)."

And then the architect did the same thing Julian himself had done a hundred times before. He simply disappeared.

Julian also went quiet. What more could he say? He didn't want to talk to us anymore. And we didn't want to talk to him, either.

That was the end. Not the end of WikiLeaks, but the end of the team that had worked so hard for the project in the years and months past. From that point on, we would only communicate with one another indirectly, via the media or go-betweens.

We gave up and began handing over responsibility for the technology. The architect helped the technician, who remained with the project to rebuild the old system. Initially, we had agreed on a transitional phase of two weeks. Ultimately, we extended it to three.

Why did the architect and I decide in the early morning hours of September 15, 2010, to quit WikiLeaks? The real question is Why didn't we make that decision much, much earlier? Perhaps we had already done so without admitting it to ourselves.

On September 17, two days after our final conversation with Julian, we registered the name of our new project: OpenLeaks.

The idea, however, was considerably older than forty-eight hours. We'd been batting it around for quite some time, in fact, and maybe it had been in the back of our minds the previous few weeks as the tone between us and Julian deteriorated. But the final decision came on September 17.

The first time either of us had said out loud that perhaps we weren't going to beat our heads against a wall at WL forever was in summer 2010. What frustrated us most were Julian's Twitter messages and the fact that we were always trying to catch up with publishing the big leaks while a lot of good documents were simply left lying around with no one to attend to them. Julian was continually announcing the next big leak, only to turn around and say he wouldn't be making any more announcements, while launching all sorts of senseless attacks on journalists in the meantime. If I recall correctly, it was immediately after Julian had heaped abuse upon the *Mother Jones* article that the architect broached the topic of us leaving. It had been a long time since a statement had filled me with such a sense of relief as the architect's casual and typically succinct message: "If thing keep going this way at WL, we'll just have to fork."

By "fork," he meant go off on our own path. Just leave. I was glad I wasn't the only one who'd had this idea. Although I knew that the architect was closer to me than to Julian, I hadn't known for sure whether, if things came to a head, he might choose to stay with WL. And the architect was crucial. Without him, it would have been virtually impossible to build up anything new.

Naturally, we encountered considerable skepticism when we began sharing our thoughts with some of the others. Harald Schumann and Birgitta were concerned that we might destroy the idea of WL itself if we split the organization. WikiLeaks, after all, was an established brand name. They urged us to resolve the problem internally, with Julian and fight to the end for WL. But the architect and I saw things more pragmatically. And no matter how much we may have hemmed and hawed, once the ice had been broken and the decisive words had been said, nothing could hold us back.

The idea fired the imaginations of Herbert, the architect, and me. At first, all we had were just vague fantasies of what a better version of WikiLeaks might be like. But soon we were mulling over names and developing ideas about how the new organization could avoid going down the same path as WL if it started attracting money and publicity. That was around July or August 2010.

We formulated the first concepts that would serve as the foundation of the new project. Some of my ideas stemmed from the time when I applied for the grant from the Knight Foundation. One of them would probably appear laughable in the eyes of more professional founders of any comparable organization. Our chief concern was how a group could make decisions without any one person imposing his will on others. Our goal was a maximum of consensus, and we preferred to discuss things for days on end rather than force everyone involved to submit to the opinion of any one person. We also wanted to avoid putting ourselves under time pressure. But if worse came to worst and no consensus could be reached, we agreed to decide issues by playing rock, paper, scissors. That would be our way of preventing situations in which any one individual would be tempted to lay down the law.

It wasn't easy to put the rock-paper-scissors principle down on paper in a way that sounded even vaguely serious. In the end, we ourselves had to laugh and deleted it from our official concept. But we did stick to the basic idea that we would create a neutral service and avoid the trap of becoming political lobbyists or pop stars. When it became clear in that final chat that we were going to leave WL, work on OpenLeaks sped up dramatically. It was a liberating experience, even if I was very sad that my time at WL was now over forever.

I also decided to go public with the news that I had left WL. It was just before the Iraq leak, and I was the one charged with keeping in touch with the journalists from *Der Spiegel*. At our next meeting I told them that, unfortunately, I was no longer their point person because I was no longer part of the WikiLeaks team.

Marcel Rosenbach and Holger Stark wanted to interview me immediately. They said that they would be able to include our conversation in their next edition. I asked for a week to think things over. I wanted to consider very carefully what to say, how much to reveal. I was aware of just how frustrated and emotional I was at that point. At all costs, I wanted to avoid letting my frustration develop into a campaign for personal revenge. I wanted my only motivation to be relativizing the credibility I had lent the project and inform people who wanted to work for WL or donate money or upload documents. In the past, I had stood up and vouched for WikiLeaks as a reliable organization. I now wanted to publicly qualify that position.

This was a new situation. For the past three years I had never told anyone what was going on inside the organization. On the contrary, I had always tried to portray WikiLeaks in the best possible light. When necessary, that involved dispelling concerns and refuting criticism. Along the way, I had indulged in a bit of spin, sometimes straddling the line between truth and propaganda. I had never, however, told a blatant lie.

I saw the two journalists from *Der Spiegel* primarily as witnesses who could attest to the legitimacy of my reservations. Whenever I met Rosenbach and Stark, they listened very attentively. During previous conversations, Stark had repeatedly pulled out his notebook. At some point I asked him why he was writing everything down. He said he wanted to be able to remember what I had said. I told him I would prefer him not to. And I reminded them of their promise not to use our internal discussions anywhere.

At one of our next meetings, Stark again had placed his notebook on the table. Maybe I'd become overly cautious, but that irritated me. There had been too many misunderstandings over the previous few weeks, too many internal details that had been made public. That's why, when I did finally give *Der Spiegel* an official interview, I was very reserved and didn't criticize Julian heavily at all.

The interview appeared on September 25. All that Monday, the day the magazine always hits newsstands, I felt nervous. I kept waiting for a reaction from Julian. But none came. The only people who contacted me were other journalists. But by that point I had no desire to talk any further about WikiLeaks and my departure from it.

I gave one or two journalists a few details about how I had quit in order to get the picture straight. Then I needed some peace and quiet.

Desperately.

19

The Iraq War Logs

O N October 22, 2010, WikiLeaks published 391,832 documents about the Iraq War. These were US military files dating from 2004 to 2009.

As had been the case with the Afghan War Diaries, the *Guardian,* the *New York Times,* and *Der Spiegel* once again enjoyed the privileged position of being able to examine the material weeks in advance and write their articles. They had been in possession of the documents since Julian had set up shop in London. The material was also posted on the WikiLeaks site on October 22, making it available to everyone. Although Julian had told me that exclusivity deals made it impossible to involve the *Washington Post* or freelance journalists, there were in fact other partners onboard this time around, including the TV stations Al Jazeera and Channel 4.

With the Afghanistan leak, David Leigh of the *Guardian* had been our main man. In the case of the Iraq release it was Gavin MacFadyen. MacFadyen is the head of the Centre for Investigative Journalism (CIJ) in London, a nonprofit organization chiefly concerned with training investigative journalists and promoting the benefits of this particularly expensive form of journalistic work.

MacFadyen also sits on the advisory board of the Bureau for Investigative Journalism, a journalists' initiative set up in 2009 that attempts, you might say, to put theory into practice. It produces four or five reports every year on particularly important topics that, in the Bureau's opinion, aren't receiving sufficient attention. The reports are not commissioned by the media industry; the Bureau itself funds the painstaking research. The Bureau is also based in London and the Centre for Investigative Journalism provides it with expert advice and reporters.

MacFadyen is both one of Julian's biggest fans and a close colleague of Iain Overton, a documentary filmmaker and the editor in chief of the Bureau. That is probably how the contact with Julian came about—and the idea to work more closely together in the run-up to the Iraq leak. Part of the idea was for the Bureau to pre-produce five-minute videos and sell the rights to them to TV stations.

In 2009 the Bureau received 2 million pounds from the Potter Foundation. Thus, it was financially independent. Its journalists were presumably interested in working together with WikiLeaks for the sake of a good story and perhaps the publicity that any association with WikiLeaks might generate.

The question of rights had already arisen with the "Collateral Murder" video. That had given Julian the idea of using the videos to tap a further source of income.

I've heard from a former *Newsweek* reporter as well as two other sources that Al Jazeera and Channel4 were among those who had paid for the five-minute clips. My sources mentioned sums of about 110,000 pounds from Al Jazeera and 50,000 pounds from Channel4. Meanwhile, Iain Overton and the Bureau, the producers of the videos, have come under fire. A number of critics have questioned whether these deals were completely kosher. They want to know whether by buying the videos the broadcasters also purchased the right to take an advance look at the documents. Overton denies this. He says the money only went toward funding his substantial production costs, and that the Bureau ended up with a loss from the deal. I have the feeling that Overton is now paying the price for dealing with a nontransparent organization.

Pre-produced videos were apparently also offered to other TV stations. Some of them, ABC for example, were suspicious about the offer and surprised by the amounts of money being asked for—100,000 pounds for five-minute TV reports. The public—including WL reporters and donors—was also left in the dark about these video sales. That is definitely a point for criticism. It remains unclear to this day who paid what and what they were promised in return. Overton has assured me that he will publicize all the background details of the deals and can show that everything was aboveboard, as far as the Bureau was concerned.

Julian would later fall out with the *Guardian,* when the paper wanted to publish some of the diplomatic cables without consulting him. According to an article by Sarah Ellison in *Vanity Fair,* Julian and his attorney stormed into the *Guardian*'s offices, claiming that the information in the documents was personal property, and that any publication would affect him financially. That raises the question: if Julian can apparently be so open about his financial interests with his media partners, why can't he make them transparent to the general public?

The media deals weren't the only new thing about the Iraq leaks. Technologically, the Iraq release also marked a departure from previous practice. The publications were hosted by an Amazon server in the United States and in Ireland, as well as on servers in France. Julian and the technician had clearly not been able to get the organization's own infrastructure back up and running to the point where it could cope with a publication of that kind. As of this writing, it is still impossible to send documents directly to WikiLeaks. The submission system is offline.

There is a page that explains what kinds of submissions WL is interested in and the technical details of the uploading procedure. The path to the site is not encrypted. Anyone reading the instructions about potential submissions can easily be monitored. Conversely, anyone who intercepts traffic between a user's computer and the Amazon server in the United States can see what information the user has accessed on the WikiLeaks site. All Internet traffic across North America can potentially be monitored by the National Security Agency. In the case of WikiLeaks, it probably is.

Upon his departure, the architect took with him almost everything he had set up and developed during his year at WikiLeaks. The software and configurations are the architect's own intellectual property. The remaining team faced the problem of how to continue without his expertise. From my perspective today, I would call the technical level of WL before the architect's arrival irresponsible—even if I did live with it myself for the first two years.

The technician could have returned WikiLeaks to the state it was at before the architect came along. The wiki could have also remained online. The architect was not responsible for programming that tool.

The architect took time to show the technician the ropes. During the handover, he led him by the hand and explained how the whole thing had to be configured. The young techie is, in fact, a really good programmer, and, as he knows, he'd be more than welcome to join our new project whenever he wants. But the rebuilding of the system was probably too much for him on his own.

Julian never seems to have taken sufficient interest in this task or given him any support. He just kept on complaining that the architect and I had destroyed everything. I don't know exactly why, as of the end of 2010, three months after our departure, the system is still not really back up on its feet. It shows that the current team is overtaxed and perhaps, to some extent at least, just not up to the job. It also shows how unsecure the system is. It has become a security risk for everyone involved. The architect did not merely remove the part of the new platform that he had programmed and installed. He and I also ensured it was safe, stored away in a neutral, secure location.

Children shouldn't play with guns. That was our argument for removing the submission platform from Julian's control. The architect, in particular, would have had moral qualms about leaving it in Julian's hands. We did not take this step to damage Julian personally. We were not motivated by revenge. And we did not want to get our own hands on the material, or divert it to Open-Leaks. We just decided to take away these dangerous toys so that Julian could not do harm to anyone else. We will only return the material to Julian if and when he can prove that he can store the material securely and handle it carefully and responsibly.

This is the first time that we've told anyone about this. We were afraid that doing so could lose us public sympathy, and perhaps that will be the result now. But I stand by this decision absolutely. We were and are primarily bound to our duty vis-à-vis our sources' security.

Julian will no doubt claim that we stole the material from him, so let me repeat this once again: We have absolutely no intention of publishing the material ourselves, even though some people keep on advising us to do just that, and even though it might be in the interests of the sources. I would never open myself up to the accusation that I had taken something that belonged to Julian Assange.

Even after our final conversation, Julian still tried to get in touch with the architect, telling him they simply had to resume working together. He said the architect should "act like a man" and "let bygones be bygones." The architect laughed at him and said, "You've missed the boat."

Julian bragged to us about his host of new staff members, his hundred new horses in the stable. But none of them have been able to get the system up and running. In Sweden, Julian allegedly had thirty or thirty-five supporters helping him for two or three weeks. I've heard they have all left because they found Julian simply too difficult.

I had been gone for a while and was already working on Open-Leaks, but I still possessed operator status. You could say that breakups in the digital world take a lot more time than in real life. If you get kicked off a sports team, you have to go play somewhere else, but I was still present in the WikiLeaks public chat room and could read all the conversations. Moreover, because I was still the operator, I could stay in the chat room without being thrown out after ten minutes of inactivity the way normal guests are. This was a precaution we had taken so that no one could listen in unnoticed.

So I saw how a personnel situation meant that the seventeen-year-old from Iceland was appointed captain of the chat. "PenguinX" was the first point of contact for anyone appearing in the chat room with a question. This is a delicate area because this is where many people who want to submit material contact the organization—all the more so because the WL e-mail hasn't worked properly since Julian refused to enter the codes to release it. Potential whistleblowers need to be warned in this situation. They should not provide any information that could identify them or do harm to others. Anyone logged on, from a curiosity seeker to a secret service agent, has access to the public chat rooms.

Moreover, after I had left, Julian assigned PenguinX to write a press release portraying me as an evil deserter of the cause. But the seventeen-year-old wasn't up to the task. He's not capable of writing a proper sentence, and he didn't know the background to the story. So he passed the job on to another volunteer, who was active in the chat room and who had offered to help.

This eager volunteer then asked me if I could help. He said he didn't understand the whole situation and would be grateful for a bit of input. My first thought was, Oh God, things really have gotten desperate. And *this* is the crack team that has its hands on documents that Julian's lawyer has described as a "thermonuclear device"?

• • •

When the nanny got in touch with me for the first time after my departure, I had to agree not to log our conversation and store it as a file. That wasn't a big problem. I typed up the transcript as best I remembered it.

I don't truly think that the nanny is an evil person, but when she told me that she only wanted to "make everyone happy," I couldn't help feeling uneasy. Our conversation was like something from a bad spy thriller. She offered to ensure that my name wasn't damaged if I agreed to stop making critical comments in public about Julian and the project. All I had to do was say yes, and in return there would be no attempts to publicly portray me in a negative light. I told her that I found her wording a little menacing. No, said the nanny, I had misunderstood. When she made threats, they were never so subtle. That wasn't her style. The nanny had tried to win back the architect with promises of a regular salary. After Birgitta left, WL tried to make her sign a confidentiality agreement.

Moreover, Julian explicitly threatened that he had some compromising material on me and that he was planning to publish e-mails in which I showed my true self. He should go ahead and do that. I have nothing to hide. Perhaps I'm just too normal a guy for that.

Julian once wrote in a chat conversation, "I'm running out of options that don't destroy people." These were the words with which he ordered Birgitta to bring us into line after our departure. That was shortly after the architect and I had left. Julian's tone was horrid, but his statement was exaggerated. I didn't feel afraid at all. It reminded me a bit of the Pentagon spokesman who appealed to us following the Afghanistan leak to "Do the right thing!" He did not reveal what exactly that was or what kind of consequences we would otherwise face. Empty threats sound serious, but in the end they're still empty.

The nanny even came to Germany and visited me at the computer club. It was on November 1, a gray Monday, and the weather was miserable. I think it was the first time that winter we had to put the heat on. I was sitting at the club's large meeting table, with my back to the wall and my eyes on the door. We spotted each other immediately.

The nanny hadn't read the *Spiegel* interview, maintaining, "I don't want to know any of that." She smiled pleasantly at me. I smiled back a little. Then she pulled out a list.

"These are the points that I'd like to clarify with you," she said.

"I haven't got much time," I said.

She read out, " 'Access codes'?" And then looked at me questioningly.

I don't think that she even knew herself what this was supposed to mean. It just sounded good. Passwords? I didn't have any passwords, or anything else. I explained to her that there had been a proper handover and that I was sorry if she had been misinformed. I really did feel sorry for her. Julian had sent her on a mission to sort out one thing or another and had told her a bunch of half-truths.

I explained why I didn't want to return the submissions

documents to Julian at this point. I asked her if she thought that things were going well at WikiLeaks. But she didn't really give me an answer.

She looked at me as if she didn't understand what language I was speaking.

I think she was flabbergasted when I stood up to leave. She wasn't used to that. Could anything be more important than a conversation with her?

I didn't want to keep my literary agent waiting. We had an appointment to work on the pitch for my book.

"Sorry, I have to go now," I said. And that was that.

20

Cablegate

THE next WL publication was the so-called cables—the dispatches written by American diplomats. They had already caused quite a lot of disruption among us.

I had always asked myself why Julian was in such a big hurry to release the documents. Julian had said his hand was forced because the Icelander had already passed on the material, but no one really seemed to understand the logic behind this. I learned later that the *Guardian* had gotten hold of the material from the freelance journalist Heather Brooke. She had copied the cables from the Icelander onto her hard drive. The *Guardian* apparently wanted to publish them independently of Julian. That story made sense. It was possible the next leak could happen without Julian Assange.

There is no way the old WL core team would have agreed to release the material at this time. Rumors began to swirl that it would appear on the final weekend of November.

At the time, Anke, Jacob, and I were visiting my parents-in-law in the countryside near Berlin. When I saw that the e-paper version of *Der Spiegel,* "for editorial reasons," was only going online on Sunday, and not as usual on Saturday, I knew what was happening. I drove back to our Berlin apartment to clean up. I got rid of everything that could attract even the slightest interest of the police—although the apartment contained nothing incriminating at all, not even a falsely calculated café bill to be deducted from my taxes. But I suspected what a search would be like. Theodor Reppe, the sponsor of the German WikiLeaks domain, had told me about how his home was searched in 2009. He'd had to explain to the officers that his subwoofer wasn't a computer. The police usually confiscate everything vaguely resembling a computer or telephone. I didn't want to have to do without my computer in the coming days. And if someone called, I wanted to be able to answer the phone.

Investigators also secure any and all documents—as far as they knew, something "thermonuclear" could be lurking at the bottom of the pile of paper waiting to be recycled in our kitchen. Or my notebook might contain the key to the WL insurance file. So I tried to rid our apartment of anything that the police might think they should take with them.

On Sunday, November 28, the first dispatches began appearing on the website Cablegate.org, which was created especially for the leak. As the site explained, the documents were confidential communiqués between the US State Department and 274 embassies around the world, dating from 1966 to late February 2010. Of 250,000, 15,652 of the dispatches were classified as "secret." Only a fraction of them, however—a few hundred in total—appeared on the Cablegate page.

The story that *Der Spiegel* made out of this material was pretty banal, focusing largely on bitchy things that US diplomats had written about world leaders: French president Nicolas Sarkozy was hypersensitive and authoritarian; Russian prime minister Vladimir Putin, an alpha male; German chancellor Angela Merkel, indecisive and uninspired; German foreign minister Guido Westerwelle, a greenhorn; and Italian prime minister Silvio Berlusconi, a vain party animal. All of them came in for a roundhouse, but the actual content was minimal. None of the dispatches were particularly shocking. The individuals with the most reason to feel insulted were those who weren't mentioned—because they weren't important enough.

The publication strategy was obvious, and I understood why *Der Spiegel* was taking it easy at the start. The 250,000 cables in total would only gradually appear on the Cablegate site. The journalists were in no hurry to make them public. The newspapers and magazines—*Der Spiegel,* the *Guardian, El País,* and *Le Monde*—wanted to exploit the material at their leisure, and if the publications continued at this pace, WL could live off them for months.

This time around, the *New York Times* was only onboard because the *Guardian* had given them the material, and I figured I knew why. The newspaper had published an unflattering article about Julian.

I can only speculate why the *Guardian* shared the material with the *Times.* They likely didn't approve of Julian's attempt to revenge himself for a negative article. And the *Guardian* probably didn't want to go it alone on the English-language market in case the publications caused legal trouble. It was good for them to have a partner in the country the writers of the dispatches came from.

The documents as they appeared on the Cablegate page were

altered. Only WikiLeaks's five exclusive media partners had access to the truly controversial details. Without doubt, it was correct to edit submissions out of the cables that contained information that could endanger individuals—our media partners had insisted we black out revealing details before documents could be published. They included the names and identifying information of Chinese dissidents and Russian or Iranian journalists who had spoken with US diplomats.

Julian agreed with this. He himself had asked the US ambassador in London to help WikiLeaks identify passages that could have put others at risk. As later reported in the media, the head lawyer of the US State Department had answered that the United States did not negotiate with people who had acquired material illegally. Julian had made a similar request of the *New York Times* with regard to the Afghanistan leaks, albeit a scant twenty-four hours before WikiLeaks published the material. He later complained that he'd gotten no help with blacking out names and revealing data.

WL's five chosen partners enjoyed a privileged position and could exploit the cables to attract more readers. That meant considerable stress for the world's remaining media outlets. They, too, had to write their articles, conduct their interviews, and film their reports. Their only option was to counter the competition's exclusives with sensationalist headlines. For instance, the German newsweekly *Stern, Der Spiegel*'s main competitor, published a pretty decent story on Bradley Manning that featured an unfortunate picture of the man within a set of superimposed sniper's crosshairs and the headline that translates into English as THIS INNOCENT LOOKING FELLOW IS HUMILIATING THE US. It was a crass and ruthless way of packaging the story, worthier of a tabloid than a serious newsmagazine.

The media also desperately needed experts they could interview and quote. Julian wasn't giving any press conferences. Sweden had issued an international warrant for his arrest, and he had gone underground. Interview requests could not be sent directly to WL because the mail server was still down. As a result, anyone with something vaguely Internet-related on his résumé could become an expert on WikiLeaks. In Germany, for instance, the blogger and social-media specialist Sascha Lobo appeared on a major political talk show to discuss WL with a public-relations advisor.

Starting on Sunday, November 28, my phone rang from morning until night. "Hello, Moscow calling. Mr. Domscheit-Berg, are you available for an interview today?" On Tuesday, it was the Japanese; on Thursday, I traveled to Cologne to appear on *Stern TV,* and on Friday, the press was lying in wait for me at a long-planned appearance I had agreed to put in at the Friedrich Naumann Foundation in Hamburg. Reporters used every trick in the book to try to make contact. They sent messages to my wife's Facebook page and called the press office of her employer. They even got in touch with the Italian restaurant around the corner from where we lived. Everyone wanted me to comment. Ideally, they wanted to hear me say how evil WL was, now that I had left the project and presumably wanted to avenge myself on Julian.

I was astonished by the number of people around this time who announced their unmitigated support for Julian Assange. *Time* magazine had placed him on their short list for Person of the Year. Mark Zuckerberg, the comparably controversial founder of

Facebook, would ultimately take that honor, but he was the editors' choice. Julian got the most votes from *Time*'s readership—bizarrely, Turkish prime minister Recep Tayyip Erdoğan came in second with readers.

I was of two minds about the people who, in the wake of the cables leak, began to attack the websites of Switzerland's PostFinance, Amazon, PayPal, MasterCard, Visa, and Moneybookers—all service providers who refused to honor contracts with WL after open hostility broke out between the project and the US State Department. The guys from Anonymous no doubt took the lead here. Their criticism of these firms was justified, and cyberattacks were their only means of getting politically involved. But they also attacked the website of the Swedish prosecutor's office, and that, to my eyes, revealed some people's inability to distinguish between political and private issues.

Journalists from all over the world were among those who came together to support Julian. The ringleader was Gavin MacFadyen of the Centre for Investigative Journalism. He posted a statement from the International Federation of Journalists expressing concern over Julian's situation: "Assange has been forced into hiding and is the subject of an international police investigation over allegations concerning sexual offences in Sweden."

After the publication of the cables, prosecutors in Australia were also examining the possibilities of criminally charging Julian. More than four thousand people signed a letter of protest, composed by two hundred prominent politicians, academics, lawyers, artists, and journalists, against the prosecutors' actions. On December 10, after Julian had turned himself in to British authorities, the *Guardian* also published an open letter signed by—among others—the Australian journalist John Pilger, the writer A. L. Kennedy, and the former ambassador and political activist Craig Murray. One section reads:

> The US government and its allies, and their friends in the media, have built up a campaign against Assange which now sees him in prison facing extradition on dubious charges, with the presumed eventual aim of ensuring his extradition to the US. We demand the immediate release, the dropping of all charges, and an end to the censorship of WikiLeaks.

On December 8, the Australian Internet organization GetUp! posted a letter of support for Julian that attracted 45,000 signatures within forty-eight hours. It called on President Obama and US Attorney General Eric Holder to stand up for the principles of innocent-until-proven-guilty and freedom of information. GetUp! announced plans to run the letter as a full-page advertisement in the *New York Times* and the *Washington Post*.

Journalist Miranda Devine, usually associated with the political right, also leaped publicly to Julian's defense, criticizing what she called the special character of the charges raised against him in Sweden and opining that no one believed he was sitting in a British jail because he was a rapist. Perhaps less surprising was the support Julian received from filmmaker Michael Moore. Moore had already contacted WL after the release of "Collateral Murder," and he was now donating the $20,000 in bail money that secured Julian's release from prison. The irony is that Julian himself always regarded the filmmaker as an idiot.

He had a similar attitude toward another of his prominent supporters, the American feminist Naomi Wolf, whose lecture series accompanying her book *Give Me Liberty: A Handbook for American Revolutionaries* Julian once dismissed as "banal stuff." Many of Julian's supporters may be stars, but I know what he really thinks of at least several of them. In his eyes, they are useful idiots, junior players, wannabes.

A lot of people probably think it's fashionable to run around sporting "Support Julian Assange" buttons and stickers. These are the same sorts of people who reflexively applaud every time the United States suffers any sort of setback.

Julian described his arrest as a witch hunt ultimately aimed at getting him extradited to the United States. When he was released on bail, his supporters inside and outside the courthouse began to cheer. Julian pumped his fists in triumph before disappearing, in electronic foot-cuffs, off to the country estate of his friend Vaughan Smith in southeast England.

Every day hordes of supporters and journalists await him outside the gates of Smith's estate. Julian has bragged that his next leak will be of tens of thousands of documents concerning the global financial crisis sufficient to bring down a bank in the United States, because the material chronicles unethical practices and grotesque legal violations. Julian has promised people a lot. Let's hope the media won't be disappointed. He has promised his fans that the pace of publications will accelerate and that WikiLeaks is invincible and able to fend off all attempts to "behead" the organization. I ask myself what material he is referring to, how he got it, and how it is being stored. I hope he's got it somewhere safe and sound.

Since the cables leak, Julian has been fearlessly aggressive in his public appearances. The nanny had long wanted to get him a PR advisor.

The formulations on the WikiLeaks website have also become more cautious. Where we used to claim "Submitting documents to WikiLeaks is safe, easy and protected by law," he now only says "Submitting documents to our journalists is protected by law in better democracies." The submissions category now also includes the statement "WikiLeaks accepts a range of material, but we do not solicit it." In addition, the word "classified" has disappeared from the "most wanted" list of materials.

When I look at recent TV and newspaper pictures of Julian, he seems a lot older. The mischievous grin he sometimes used to flash is gone. He seems slicker and better-looking, more like the head of a company. I liked him a lot better when he sported a backpack and old blue jeans.

I was invited to appear on *Stern TV* in Germany, which gave me a chance to experience the media circus from the other side.

Before the show I waited around in the greenroom. With me was a fellow guest, the former Swiss ambassador to Germany, Thomas Borer. He's known chiefly for the false accusations of an extramarital affair with a model that German tabloids made about him in 2002. Borer came over to me and introduced himself with the words "I really admire people who show civic courage." How nice of him, I thought—until he added, "That's something people have often said about me, too." Borer's tone was relaxed, statesmanlike. His chest was puffed out a bit, and his voice had the most sonorous tone he could manage.

We then went to the dressing room of the host, Günther Jauch, to discuss the show. Borer and I took our seats, and I prepared myself for a couple of questions from one of Germany's best-known entertainment journalists. I flattered myself that I was somewhat different from Jauch's usual guests, and I figured he would relish the opportunity to talk about something truly substantial. But after two or three sentences, the plans for the show were over: I'll ask you something, and then you, and then we'll have a discussion. That dealt with, Borer and Jauch began to talk about a topic closer to their hearts—real-estate prices for lakefront property in Zürich and Berlin.

I was bored out of my mind. The outside world was full of news about some potentially very significant diplomatic revelations, and here in Jauch's dressing room we were talking about how much a waterfront view was worth.

In general, the media wanted me to repudiate WL. I was cautious. The more generic and neutral my answers were, the more leading the questions asked by journalists became. I tried to resist their lures. What the debate about WikiLeaks continues to lack is a differentiated analysis of the various points of criticism. That's too complicated to be packed into media-friendly sound bites.

Of course Julian deserves support. Above all, we Europeans have to prevent him from being extradited to the United States, where some people have called for him to face the death penalty. That would set a terrible precedent, and we can't allow it to happen. On the other hand, I don't understand how people can object to him facing a regular court in Sweden.

The charges against him have nothing to do with WikiLeaks. They're about Julian as a private person and two women, and he should face those accusations. If he doesn't, it would be a clear abuse of power—the sort of abuse WikiLeaks tries to prevent where other people are concerned.

Julian once said something very revealing in an Australian documentary. He had just appeared on *Larry King Live,* and his face was all over the covers of international newspapers and magazines. Lost in what seemed to be a narcissistic daydream, Julian muttered, "Now I am untouchable in this country." The journalist who was interviewing Julian did a double take.

"That's a bit of hubris," he said.

"Well, for a couple of days," Julian added.

No one should be untouchable. Not even Julian Assange. I cannot understand how anyone else can support this idea, even for a second.

I hope that everyone concerned gets a fair trial in Sweden, and I don't see any reason to believe otherwise. Sweden is not known for its hanging judges, its susceptibility to American influence, or a judicial system that lacks transparency. If Julian is innocent, and I presume he is unless and until the opposite is proven, he has nothing to fear.

The Australian police have meanwhile suspended the investigations concerning WL, having been unable to find any violation of Australian law. The situation is different in the United States, however, where efforts are still being made to drag WL and its supporters in front of the courts and hinder further publications.

American legal experts differ as to whether American laws allow for charges to be brought in this regard, and whether, if that is the case, the United States would also have to charge the periodicals that published WL material. The latter would appear to contradict the guarantee of freedom of speech in the First Amendment to the Constitution.

Ironically, Julian could potentially be charged under the Espionage Act he was so fond of quoting to us. In order for that to happen, though, the US attorney general would have to show that Julian intentionally acted in such a way as to damage the United States. I can't imagine how this could be proven. I'm no legal expert, but I think any resulting trial would be both absurd and undemocratic.

At present, American prosecutors are concentrating on showing that Julian actively solicited certain information, which would mean he could be charged as an accomplice to our sources. That might benefit Bradley Manning, the man who may or may not have been the source behind the leaked military documents. If Julian did play an active role in soliciting this leak, he would have violated one of WikiLeaks's core principles.

On the other hand, I am fundamentally opposed to anyone facing legal sanction for making information public. Instituting legal protections to this end, which is the basic idea of the IMMI, is a cause that all journalists, publishers, politicians, and concerned citizens should support. Moreover, I remain in favor of publishing the cables. The decision to do so was both correct and important, and I would leap to the defense of anyone involved in the publication.

A lot has been written, especially in newspapers that are not privileged partners of WL, that the cables contained no real information. That makes me ask what people think is important other than sports scores and celebrity gossip. Is it really so totally uninteresting that a Lebanese defense minister would hope for Israel to bomb his country so his government could move against Hezbollah? I think it's also worth knowing that in addition to undermining the political authority of the United Nations, the United States also systematically spies on UN members. That Secretary of State Hillary Clinton asked her diplomats to collect information on top UN figures, including their e-mail passwords, health information, and credit card numbers. Or that a former vice president of Afghanistan was caught with a suitcase containing $52 million in Dubai but got off scot-free. I find this interesting—not least because I ask myself how the man managed to fit so much money in a suitcase to begin with.

As a German citizen, I'm also interested in the fact that Helmut Metzner, a high-ranking official in the Free Democrats' party headquarters, was passing on information to Washington. God knows, I've read a lot more pointless stuff in newspapers. People who say that everyone knows politicians lie and deceive and spy and bribe are only giving themselves an excuse for not getting involved in politics. Do people refuse to watch the nightly news just because everybody knows that wars are going on all over the world, or that people often aren't very nice to one another?

I have even less sympathy for those backward-looking defenders of nontransparency who are always telling the world that some things need to be kept secret. We in the West have a long and unworthy tradition of choking off attempts at public discussion with reference to some "greater good" that needs to be protected.

I have yet to hear a convincing argument for why this should be the case. I am convinced that citizens not only can, but must be burdened with the truth. Why shouldn't the German public, for instance, be aware that their nation's military is involved in a number of wars around the world? Why should people be protected from knowing about global machinations and problems? Arguments to the contrary are paternalistic, elitist bullshit, and I think it's very reasonable to fight for increased transparency and equal access to knowledge for all.

Nonetheless, I do have a couple of problems with how the cables are being published. The first concerns the role of WL's exclusive media partners. Writer and professor of political theory Herfried Münkler published an article in *Der Spiegel* criticizing the fact that they appeared at all. I don't agree with much that Münkler wrote, but on one important point he was right: Someone who criticizes the fact that secrets always remain in the hands of a chosen few with power must answer the question of whether his publishing strategy truly makes them accessible to everyone. Is it not the case, as Münkler asked, that with the cables only the guardians of the secrets are being replaced?

Confidential information once kept under wraps by the US State Department and the American military is now in the hands of five large media companies and Julian Assange. *They* decide what is of public interest and what is not. The recent Cablegate publications are a far cry from the original ideas behind WikiLeaks. I think they stray much too far from those basic principles.

What's more, people are now apparently traveling the world offering unreleased dispatches to other media outlets. One of these people is Johannes Wahlström from Sweden. Wahlström is the son of Israel Shamir, a notorious anti-Semite and Holo-caust denier of Russian-Israeli extraction. Kristinn Hrafnsson, WL's new official spokesman, has described both Wahlström and Shamir as belonging to WL. I think Julian is aware of the sort of people he's associating himself with—there's been contact with Shamir, at least, for years. When Julian first learned about Shamir's political background, he considered whether he might be able to work for WikiLeaks under a pseudonym. Once, he described to me things Shamir had written as "very clever really." This is not to say Julian is anti-Semitic. In my experience, he was critical of Israel, but his criticism was always directed solely at the Israeli government. So I have no clue why he tolerates a notorious anti-Semite in his immediate environment.

From the outside, it looks as through Wahlström has passed on the cables to various media outlets in Scandinavia while his father has assumed responsibility for the Russian market. Although WL's five chosen media partners have repeatedly denied buying access to the leaks, the Norwegian newspaper *Aftenposten* outright admitted to paying for a look at the cables. All the other news-papers, including some Russian ones, have refused to provide any information about possible deals with WL.

What I find even worse than exchanging money for leaks, though, is the possibility that someone could use them for non-journalistic purposes. Or the chance that someone could purchase exclusive access to documents with the express intent of ensuring that they never see the light of day. It wouldn't be the first time documents were kept under lock and key because someone feared what they had to say.

21

The Promise of
OpenLeaks

T HE architect and I registered the domain for our new project on September 17, 2010, two days after we left WikiLeaks. We had long been thinking about how the whistle-blower platform of the future should be, the kind of things it should be capable of. It was one of the things I had worked on, for example, with one of our supporters for our application to the Knight Foundation.

We had kept Julian regularly informed, but he hadn't seemed all that interested. Julian had his own ideas about how WL should develop. He wanted to release one leak after another, as aggressively as possible, and generate a maximum of conflict. He seemed to have no interest in content or further technological development. Probably he was just not the sort of person who plans for the long-term future.

The real problem with WikiLeaks is that it tried to do too many things at once. WL encompassed the entire whistle-blowing process. The sources uploaded the documents; WL members erased the metadata, verified the submissions, and provided the context in additional texts. In the end, everything was put on the WL site.

At some point, it became impossible to do all these jobs adequately. There were simply too many documents coming in. That would have taken hundreds of deeply involved volunteers. So we were compelled to make choices. Which leaks should see the light of day, and which ones would lie unpublished on servers spread across the world? We were overwhelmed. This was no doubt very disappointing for would-be whistle-blowers who are still waiting to see the rewards of their courage and hoping for changes that would gradually improve our society.

Every selection process involves a kind of censorship, and every instance of censorship has a political component. It begins with the people involved agreeing to solicit public attention for a certain topic. And no one would deny anymore that WL attracts public attention. Because one person, Julian Assange, held too many of the strings, WikiLeaks became a global political player—something it was never intended to be. That spelled the end of our pledge to maintain strict neutrality—one of WL's most important principles.

At some point, we all realized that we would have to find partners. But Julian alone wanted to decide which media outlets we cooperated with. By all indications, he also later tried to cut out publications when he didn't like what they reported. It was an indirect attempt to force journalists to write positive things about WikiLeaks. The conflicts with journalists have left behind a lot of scorched earth. It shows clearly that this sort of approach doesn't work.

For a long time I had asked myself whether any single platform could ever meet the needs of all the various people concerned. WL received documents from all over the world about the most diverse subjects; everything from American foreign policy to East Timor and Kenya on down to a building-permits office in a small town. Was the solution really to have a single platform for all of this? We had become a five-and-dime store or, even worse, a giant supermarket for secret documents. But in terms of our expertise and resources we were more like a small specialty IT firm.

It was much wiser to concentrate on strengths. Our new approach is to offer only the technical infrastructure for whistle-blowers. That also reduces the likelihood that any one individual has too much power within the system.

At OL, we're taking a new path, sharing responsibility and distributing the burden to many shoulders—ideally using the people best suited for the particular task.

Separating the receipt and publication of documents would not only solve the problem of centralization, it would also prevent OpenLeaks from beginning to exert political influence of its own. The information and the decisions about what to do with it should be in the hands of those who have experience in these areas.

The media could take over the publication of documents leaked to OL, but so too could NGOs, trade unions, or other organizations devoted to making things publicly transparent. They all had experience with documents that were kept under lock and key. They knew how to deal with them, could evaluate them professionally and decide what should be published in what form—either as a report or a complete collection of documents.

We have also uncovered decisions about which potential Open-Leaks partners should receive documents from external influences.

For us there is only one person who could legitimately make this decision: the source.

At OpenLeaks, if sources think that something is best suited to the local press, they have the right to see that this happens. If they believe Amnesty International is the best recipient, OL will honor their decision. This idea had been one of the central points of our application to the Knight Foundation. At OL we put it into practice. And this will ensure that information gets to wherever it can have an effect. Depending on the material in question, that might be a news outlet, a specialized NGO, or a trade union. Who knows better than the sources themselves? That was the only way that leaks of regional significance—for example, poisonous food supplies—could attract attention alongside more spectacular documents with global import. At OpenLeaks we don't have to choose between lots of small leaks and a few big ones. There's a place in the system for them all.

Unlike WikiLeaks, OpenLeaks is not a publishing platform. It concentrates entirely on the first half of the whistle-blowing process, ensuring that documents can be submitted securely and that those they are addressed to can work with them. Like WL, OpenLeaks does this via a kind of protected mailbox into which the whistle-blower can deposit documents intended for specific recipients. We will be offering a whole series of such digital mailboxes—for every one of our partners.

The source can not only choose a recipient from the partners with OL mailboxes, he or she can also decide how long the recipient has exclusive access to the documents. After that interval has expired, if the source so desires, the submission is opened up to other OpenLeaks participants. This mechanism guarantees that a submission can't be simply suppressed.

It would be naive to think that newspapers, most of which are financed largely by advertising, are fully free in their decisions about what to publish. There are enough examples of companies yanking ads if they don't like an article about their products or management. We hope that by enlisting the broadest possible pool of participants, there will always be someone to publish important information. The interest among our potential partner organizations has been great. They include those publications that have worked together closely with WL in the past. And there are also a lot of sources who want to entrust us with their documents.

We hope a broad base will have a protective effect on the entire OpenLeaks community. A large network of partners—media outlets, NGOs, trade unions, journalism schools, and other independent organizations—would be a strong bulwark against attacks on the principle of digital mailboxes. The right to receive information and documents from anonymous sources should apply just as much to the digital world as to the traditional mail.

If a lot of strong partners from various segments of society and the media are involved, it will be very advantageous. Together they will do everything they can to prevent the enemies of digital whistle-blowing from derailing this principle.

At the start, we intend to work with only a handful of media outlets and then expand our circle of partners one by one. We want to take our time so that we can analyze how our construct works in practice and optimize it. The first tests are planned for the first half of 2011. We don't want to take off like a rocket. We want to take the time to do things right.

OpenLeaks is not a rival to WikiLeaks. We're not going to publish anything ourselves. We're not going to touch the several thousands of documents submitted to WL that we are keeping in a safe environment. At most, we'll appeal to sources who are still waiting for their documents to be published to submit them to one of our partners.

As far as we're concerned, WikiLeaks should continue to publish material, to grow, and to flourish. But we also think that WL should not be the only platform of its type for global whistle-blowing in the digital age. There's enough injustice in the world to occupy more than one platform.

Thankfully, there's no "founder" at OpenLeaks. I never want to have to discuss this issue again. A lot of people have contributed to the development of the idea, and they are all originators. The same applies to everyone who is now helping to establish OL. Along with the architect and Herbert, a couple of old friends from WL have now joined OpenLeaks. People from around the world are getting in touch, offering to share their expertise with the project. The community is wide-awake and eager to work for a good cause. And that's the way it should be!

Of course, not everyone at OpenLeaks always agrees, and there are a lot of discussions. A lot of the people working for OL have strong personalities. It is clear we will need more established internal structures to determine who will decide what, and who is responsible for which areas. Are we going to end up playing rock, paper, scissors to remain able to act, if we don't manage to reach a consensus on an especially controversial question? Even if we start out trying to do without hard-and-fast rules, we learned at WL that you can't put off the issue indefinitely. And though it may not sound all that spectacular, what I really enjoy is seeing that everyone compromises sometimes when we encounter internal disagreements.

In 2011 we also plan to help set up a charitable foundation, intended not just to promote OL but to support other work as well. We are presently experiencing a cultural transformation; we've barely left the cradle in terms of freedom of information and whistle-blowing on the Internet. The foundation will address the questions that arise and develop future-oriented models for the digital revelation of secrets. We hope to convince experts from a variety of areas—politics, society, and science—to serve on the foundation's board of advisors. And the foundation itself will also be transparent. Transparency needs a strong lobby.

In addition we want to share our knowledge—this is probably the most important part of the undertaking. We intend to record our experiences and deposit them in a public database and hope to enlist volunteers from around the world. The database will hopefully contain information about laws concerning whistle-blower protection as well as legal precedents in various countries. This information should allow whistle-blowers or group initiatives to protect themselves as much as possible. Anyone interested in promoting transparency from the bottom up will be able to get needed information.

WikiLeaks's prominence—which was due mostly to Julian,

but also to all our hard work—made the topic of whistle-blowing socially acceptable. Questions about people's right to keep secrets and reveal confidential information have become part of mainstream society. The hype surrounding WikiLeaks made a significant contribution to this. But we need to get beyond the hype and tackle the real issues and underlying questions. We shouldn't fixate on vivid magazine stories or bold-print headlines. A lot of worthy stories about the leaks remain obscured behind reports focused on sleazy personal connections.

OpenLeaks can be seen as a kind of sober, neutral infrastructure. We see ourselves as technological engineers, not as media stars or global galactic saviors. Some people may even think we're boring. That's just how we want to be. The main thing is that the system works.

TODAY, in January 2011, I'm at much the same point as I was a year ago, when we thought it would be possible to reestablish WL on a new footing. With OpenLeaks, we're trying to build up something we believe is the best way to solve a few of the world's problems. If 2010 was the year of media hype, 2011, we hope, will be the year of substance.

As I was writing my story, new facts were revealed and some of my questions were answered. At the same time, the picture of WikiLeaks's actual situation has become increasingly opaque. We are flooded by media information, and this encourages conspiracy theories, rumors, and myths, creating confusion and deflecting attention from the genuine issues.

In order to dispel the confusion and clear up the mysteries surrounding WL, we need answers to certain questions. They include:

- What is WikiLeaks's financial situation? What have donations been used for? And who decides how money is allocated?

- What is the current organizational and decision-making structure? How are responsibilities divided up?
- What did Julian mean when he reportedly told the *Guardian* that he had a financial interest in how and when the diplomatic cables were published?
- What roles do WL's representatives in Russia and Scandinavia, Israel Shamir and Johannes Wahlström, a father an son with a record of anti-Semitism, play at WikiLeaks?
- What kinds of deals have Wahlström and Shamir arranged with media outlets?
- Are there other WL brokers who have provided media outlets with material, and if so, on what terms?
- Do Julian Assange, other people involved with WikiLeaks, or their companies profit from any such deals?

Only when the specific facts are sorted out will we understand how things have come to be the way they are. Only then can we answer the question of what went wrong with WikiLeaks and the brilliant idea of using a state-of-the-art tool to make matters of urgent public concern truly transparent.

Our society needs citizens capable of thinking and acting on their own. People who do not shy away from critical questions because they're afraid of being disappointed. Our society needs individuals who are able to distinguish good information from bad and to make good decisions based on that knowledge, instead of relinquishing all personal responsibility to messiahs, leaders, and alpha wolves.

I have often been asked if my departure from WikiLeaks was disillusioning. I always answered in the affirmative. In the beginning, I was particularly disillusioned in an emotional sense. But in the past few weeks, especially in the course of working on this book, I came to realize that disillusionment also means being freed from illusions. That is constructive. It helps you to better understand your reality. And that, perhaps, is a truly good omen.

Acknowledgments

A LOT of people are responsible for the existence of this book and the story behind it, and I would like to give my thanks especially to:

Tina Klopp for sharing two productive months and writing out all my stories in such a short time.

My editor, Silvie Horch, and the rest of the excellent team at Econ Books, without whose expertise and flexibility there would have been no way this book could have been published so quickly.

My agent, Barbara Wenner, for her first-rate assistance from the genesis of this book to its publication and beyond.

The colleagues at the foreign publishers who translated this book so that it could be published in seventeen countries thus far. In particular, Charlie Conrad from Crown Publishers in America for valuable feedback on the book's content.

The attorneys Markus Kompa and Dr. Sven Krüger, as well as Amanda Telfer and Matthew Martin, for invaluable feedback on the content.

My family, for giving me the values that make me who I am.

My wife, Anke, who is my equal, and my son, Jacob.

The Chaos Computer Club and its chaotic members, for too many things to list.

The makers of Club-Mate. What would I be without you? Probably very tired.

The Internet, for always striking back.

Everyone who was directly or indirectly involved in the WL show over the past three years. Without you, nothing would have been possible.

The numerous sources whose material we published. If a few more people had your courage, the world would be a much better place.

Julian Assange, for manifesting an idea and bringing it into my life.

The OpenLeaks team, for keeping up the good work!

About the Authors

DANIEL DOMSCHEIT-BERG is a computer scientist who worked in IT security prior to devoting himself full-time to WikiLeaks. He remains committed to freedom of information on the Internet. Today he and other former WikiLeaks people are working on a more transparent secret-sharing website called OpenLeaks to be launched in early 2011. He lives in Berlin with his family.

TINA KLOPP was born in 1976 in Hamburg. She received a degree from the German School of Journalism in Munich and was the recipient of the Friedwart Bruckhaus Prize in 2006 and the 2010 Radio Play Prize of the German Literary Foundation. She currently works as a journalist at *Zeit Online*.

A Note on the Type

This book was set in Adobe Garamond, a typeface designed by Robert Slimbach in 1989. It is based on Claude Garamond's sixteenth-century type samples found at the Plantin-Moretus Museum in Antwerp, Belgium.